Synthesis Lectures on Ocean Systems Engineering

Series Editor

Nikolas Xiros, University of New Orleans, New Orleans, USA

The series publishes short books on state-of-the-art research and applications in related and interdependent areas of design, construction, maintenance and operation of marine vessels and structures as well as ocean and oceanic engineering.

Alexander Arnfinn Olsen · Fidaa Karkori

Ship's Officer's Guide to Port State Control

Responsibilities and Procedures

Alexander Arnfinn Olsen
Southampton, UK

Fidaa Karkori ⓘ
Southampton, UK

ISSN 2692-4420   ISSN 2692-4471 (electronic)
Synthesis Lectures on Ocean Systems Engineering
ISBN 978-3-031-77501-7   ISBN 978-3-031-77502-4 (eBook)
https://doi.org/10.1007/978-3-031-77502-4

This title is published with the kind permission of the American Bureau of Shipping.

© The Editor(s) (if applicable) and The Author(s), under exclusive license to Springer Nature Switzerland AG 2025

This work is subject to copyright. All rights are solely and exclusively licensed by the Publisher, whether the whole or part of the material is concerned, specifically the rights of translation, reprinting, reuse of illustrations, recitation, broadcasting, reproduction on microfilms or in any other physical way, and transmission or information storage and retrieval, electronic adaptation, computer software, or by similar or dissimilar methodology now known or hereafter developed.
The use of general descriptive names, registered names, trademarks, service marks, etc. in this publication does not imply, even in the absence of a specific statement, that such names are exempt from the relevant protective laws and regulations and therefore free for general use.
The publisher, the authors and the editors are safe to assume that the advice and information in this book are believed to be true and accurate at the date of publication. Neither the publisher nor the authors or the editors give a warranty, expressed or implied, with respect to the material contained herein or for any errors or omissions that may have been made. The publisher remains neutral with regard to jurisdictional claims in published maps and institutional affiliations.

This Springer imprint is published by the registered company Springer Nature Switzerland AG
The registered company address is: Gewerbestrasse 11, 6330 Cham, Switzerland

If disposing of this product, please recycle the paper.

Definitions

Bulk carrier: While noting the definitions in SOLAS 1974, regulations IX/1.6 and XII/1.1 and resolution MSC.277(85), for the purposes of Port State Control, Port State Control Officers should be guided by the vessel's type indicated in the vessel's certificates in determining whether a vessel is a bulk carrier and recognise that a vessel which is not designated as a bulk carrier as the vessel type on the vessel certificate may carry certain bulk cargo as provided for in the above instruments.

Clear grounds: Evidence that the vessel, its equipment, or its crew do not correspond substantially with the requirements of the relevant conventions or that the vessel's master or crew members are not familiar with essential shipboard procedures relating to the safety of vessels or the prevention of pollution.

Deficiency: A condition found not to be compliant with the requirements of the relevant convention.

Detention: Intervention action taken by the Port State when the condition of the vessel or its crew does not correspond substantially with the relevant conventions to ensure that the vessel will not sail until it can proceed to sea without presenting a danger to the vessel or persons on board, or without presenting an unreasonable threat of harm to the marine environment, whether such action will affect the normal schedule of the departure of the vessel.

Initial inspection: A visit on board a vessel to check the validity of the relevant certificates and other documents, the overall condition of the vessel, its equipment and its crew.

More detailed inspection: An inspection conducted when there are "clear grounds", as defined above.

Nearest appropriate and available repair yard: A port where follow-up action can be taken, and it is in, or closest to, the port of detention or the port where the vessel is authorised to proceed accounting for the cargo on board.

Port State Control Officer (PSCO): A person duly authorised by the competent authority of a Party to a relevant convention to carry out Port State Control inspections, and responsible exclusively to that Party.

Recognised organisation (RO): An organisation that meets the relevant conditions set forth in the Code for Recognised Organisations (RO Code) (MSC.349(92) and MEPC.237(65)) and has been assessed and authorised by the Flag State Administration in accordance with provisions of the RO Code to provide the necessary statutory services and certification to vessels entitled to fly its Flag.

Stoppage of an operation: Formal prohibition against a vessel to continue an operation due to an identified deficiency or deficiencies which, unilaterally or together, render the continuation of such operation hazardous.

Substandard vessel: A vessel whose hull, machinery, equipment or operational safety is substantially below the standards required by the relevant convention or whose crew is not in conformity with the safe manning document.

Valid certificates: A certificate that has been issued, electronically or on paper, directly by a Party to a relevant convention or on its behalf by an RO, contains accurate and effective dates, meets the provisions of the relevant convention and to which the particulars of the vessel, its crew and its equipment correspond.

Contents

1 Port State Control Regime 1
   1.1 Application and Scope 1
        1.1.1 Provision for Port State Control 3
        1.1.2 Vessels of Non-parties 3
        1.1.3 Vessels Below Conventional Size 4
        1.1.4 Professional Profile of Port State Control Officer ... 4
        1.1.5 Qualification and Training Requirements for Port State Control Officers 5
   1.2 Port State Inspections 5
        1.2.1 Initial Inspections 6
        1.2.2 General Procedural Guidelines for Port State Control Officers 7
        1.2.3 Clear Grounds 9
        1.2.4 More Detailed Inspections 9
   1.3 Contravention and Detention 10
        1.3.1 Identification of a Substandard Vessel 10
        1.3.2 Submission of Information Concerning Deficiencies ... 10
        1.3.3 Port State Action in Response to Alleged Substandard Vessels 11
        1.3.4 Responsibilities of Port State to Take Remedial Action ... 11
        1.3.5 Guidance for the Detention of Vessels 12
        1.3.6 Suspension of Inspection 12
        1.3.7 Procedures for Rectification of Deficiencies and Release ... 12
   1.4 Reporting and Review Requirements 13
        1.4.1 Port State Reporting 13
        1.4.2 Flag State Reporting 14
        1.4.3 Reporting of Allegations Under MARPOL 14
   1.5 Review Procedures 15

2	**Conduct of Port State Control Officers**		17
	2.1	Conduct of Port State Control Officers	18
		2.1.1 Actions and Behaviours Expected of Port State Control Officers	18
3	**Detention of Vessels**		21
	3.1	Principles Governing Rectification of Deficiencies or Detention of a Vessel	21
		3.1.1 Detention Related to Minimum Safe Manning and STCW Certification	21
		3.1.2 Procedures for the Detention of Vessels of All Sizes	22
		3.1.3 Invalid Certificates	23
		3.1.4 Detainable Deficiencies	23
		3.1.5 Areas Which May not Warrant a Detention, but Where, for Example, Cargo Operations Should be Suspended	28
4	**Conduct of Investigations and Inspections Under MARPOL Annex I**		29
	4.1	Inspection of the IOPP Certificate, Vessel and Equipment	29
		4.1.1 Vessels Required to Carry an IOPP Certificate	29
		4.1.2 Vessels of Non-parties to MARPOL Annex I and Other Vessels not Required to Carry an IOPP Certificate	30
		4.1.3 Control	30
	4.2	Contravention of the Discharge Provisions	31
	4.3	Itemised List of Possible Evidence on Alleged Contravention of the MARPOL Annex I Discharge Provisions	32
		4.3.1 Action on Sighting Oil Pollution	32
		4.3.2 Investigation on Board	34
		4.3.3 Investigation Ashore	36
	4.4	In-Port Inspection of Crude Oil Washing Procedures	37
		4.4.1 Inspection Requirements	37
		4.4.2 Wash Programmes	39
		4.4.3 Stripping of Tanks	40
		4.4.4 Ballasting	40
5	**Investigations and Inspections Carried Out Under MARPOL Annex II**		43
	5.1	Inspection of Certificate (COF or NLS Certificate), Vessel and Equipment	43
		5.1.1 Vessels Required to Hold a Certificate	43
		5.1.2 Vessels of Non-parties to the Convention	44
		5.1.3 Control	45

	5.2	Contravention of Discharge Provisions	45
	5.3	Itemised List of Possible Evidence on Alleged Contravention of the MARPOL Annex II Discharge Provisions	46
		5.3.1 Action on Sighting Pollution	46
		5.3.2 Investigation on Board	48
		5.3.3 Investigation Ashore	49
	5.4	Conclusion	50
	5.5	Procedures for Inspection of Unloading, Stripping and Prewashing Operations (Mainly in Unloading Ports)	50
		5.5.1 Documentation	50
		5.5.2 Information by Vessel's Staff	51
		5.5.3 Information from Terminal Staff	51
		5.5.4 Control	51
6	**Discharge Requirements Under MARPOL Annexes I and II**		**55**
	6.1	Port State Action	57
	6.2	Inspection of Crude Oil Washing Operations	57
	6.3	Inspection of Unloading, Stripping and Prewash Operations	58
7	**More Detailed Inspections for Vessel Structural and Equipment Requirements**		**61**
	7.1	Considerations for Detailed Inspections	61
		7.1.1 Conditions of the Vessel's Structure	61
		7.1.2 Conditions of Machinery Spaces	62
		7.1.3 Conditions of Assignment of Load Lines	63
		7.1.4 Lifesaving Appliances	63
		7.1.5 Fire Safety	64
		7.1.6 Application of the Regulations for Preventing Collisions at Sea (COLREGs)	65
		7.1.7 Cargo Ship Safety Construction Certificate	65
		7.1.8 Cargo Ship Safety Radio Certificates	65
		7.1.9 Means of Access to Vessel	66
		7.1.10 Equipment in Excess of Convention or Flag State Requirements	66
8	**Control of Operational Requirements**		**67**
	8.1	Inspection Processes	67
		8.1.1 Definitions and Abbreviations	68
	8.2	More Detailed Inspection for Operational Requirements	68
		8.2.1 Drills	68
		8.2.2 Meeting on Inspection Outcomes and Findings with Respect to Operational Requirements	69
		8.2.3 Communication	69

		8.2.4	Assessing the Vessel with Respect to Operational Requirements	70
		8.2.5	Detailed Guidance on Assessing Compliance with Operational Requirements	71
		8.2.6	Witnessing and Assessment of Drills	72
		8.2.7	Detention Under Operational Requirements	73
	8.3	Specific Inspection Activities		73
		8.3.1	Bridge Operation	74
		8.3.2	Cargo Operation	74
		8.3.3	Operation of Machinery	75
		8.3.4	Manuals, Instructions, etc.	77
		8.3.5	Oil and Oily Mixtures from Machinery Spaces	77
		8.3.6	Loading, Unloading and Cleaning Procedures for Cargo Spaces of Tankers	78
		8.3.7	Dangerous Goods and Harmful Substances in Packaged Form	79
		8.3.8	Garbage	80
		8.3.9	Sewage	80
		8.3.10	Air Pollution Prevention	81
	8.4	Specific Guidance		81
		8.4.1	Muster List	81
		8.4.2	Communication During Drills	82
		8.4.3	Search and Rescue Plan	83
		8.4.4	Fire and Abandon Ship Drills	83
		8.4.5	Fire Drills	84
		8.4.6	Abandon Ship Drills	85
		8.4.7	Enclosed Space Entry and Rescue Drills	86
		8.4.8	Emergency Steering Drills	86
		8.4.9	Damage Control Plan and Shipboard Oil Pollution Emergency Plan (SOPEP) or Shipboard Marine Pollution Emergency Plan (SMPEP)	87
		8.4.10	Fire Control Plan	87
9	**ISM Code**			89
	9.1	Relevant Documentation		90
	9.2	Definitions and Abbreviations		90
	9.3	Inspection of Vessel		91
		9.3.1	Initial Inspection	91
		9.3.2	Clear Grounds	92
		9.3.3	More Detailed Inspection	93

	9.4	Follow-Up Action	93
		9.4.1 Technical, Operational and ISM Code Deficiencies	93
		9.4.2 Deficiencies not Warranting Detention	94
		9.4.3 Deficiencies Warranting Detention	94
	9.5	Reporting	95
		9.5.1 Technical and Operational-Related Deficiencies	95
		9.5.2 ISM Deficiency	95
10		Port State Control Procedures Related to LRIT	97
	10.1	Inspection of Vessels Required to Carry LRIT Equipment	98
		10.1.1 Initial Inspection	98
		10.1.2 Clear Grounds	98
		10.1.3 More Detailed Inspection	99
		10.1.4 Deficiencies Warranting Detention	99
11		**Port State Control Under Tonnage 1969**	101
12		**Certification of Seafarers, Manning and Hours of Rest**	103
	12.1	Relevant Documentation	104
		12.1.1 Seafarer Certification	104
		12.1.2 Manning	104
		12.1.3 Hours of Rest	104
	12.2	Definitions and Abbreviations	104
	12.3	Inspection of the Vessel	105
		12.3.1 Pre-Boarding Preparation	105
		12.3.2 Initial Inspection	105
		12.3.3 Manning	107
		12.3.4 Hours of Rest	108
		12.3.5 Clear Grounds	109
		12.3.6 More Detailed Inspection	110
	12.4	Follow-Up Action	111
		12.4.1 Possible Action	111
		12.4.2 Possible Deficiencies	111
		12.4.3 Deficiencies That May Warrant Detention	112
		12.4.4 Actions to Be Considered	113
	12.5	Note on Reporting Deficiencies	114
13		**Port State Control Inspections Under MARPOL Annex VI**	115
	13.1	Inspections of Vessels Required to Carry the IAPP Certificate and/or the IEE Certificate	115
		13.1.1 Initial Inspections	115
		13.1.2 Initial Inspection on Vessels Equipped with Equivalent Means of SO_x Compliance	118

	13.1.3	Initial Inspection Within an Emission Control Area	118
	13.1.4	Initial Inspection Outside an ECA or First Port After Transiting an ECA	119
13.2	Outcome of Initial Inspection		120
13.3	More Detailed Inspections		121
13.4	Detainable Deficiencies		124
13.5	Inspections of Vessels of Non-parties to the Annex and Other Vessels not Required to Carry the IAPP Certificate or the IEE Certificate		125
	13.5.1	Vessels of Non-parties and Vessels not Required to Carry the IAPP Certificate	125
	13.5.2	Vessels of Non-parties and Vessels not Required to Carry the IEE Certificate	126
	13.5.3	Claims of Non-availability of Compliant Fuel Oil	126

Annex A 129

Abbreviations and Acronyms

ADA	Alternative design and arrangements
AFS	Anti-fouling System
AIS	Automatic Identification System
ASP	Application Service Provider
BDN	Bunker Delivery Notes
BWM	Ballast water management
CLC 1969	International Convention on Civil Liability for Oil Pollution Damage, 1969
CLC PROT 1992	International Convention on Civil Liability for Oil Pollution Damage, 1969, as amended
CO_2	Carbon Dioxide
CoC	Certificate of Competency
COF	Certificate of Fitness
COLREG 1972	Convention on the International Regulations for Preventing Collisions at Sea, 1972
CoP	Certificate of Proficiency
COW	Crude oil washing
CRA	Confirmation of Receipt of Application
CRB	Cargo Record Book
CSS	Code of Safe Practice for Cargo Stowage and Securing
DOC	Document of Compliance
DSC	Digital Selective Calling
ECA	Emission Control Area
ECDIS	Electronic Chart Display and Information System
EGCS	Exhaust Gas Cleaning System
EIAPP	Engine International Air Pollution Prevention Certificates
EOW	Engineer of the Watch

ESP 2011	International Code on the Enhanced Programme of Inspections during Surveys of Bulk Carriers and Oil Tankers, 2011
ETM	Exhaust Gas Cleaning (EGC) System Technical Manual
ETM-A	Exhaust Gas Cleaning (EGC) System—Technical Manual for Scheme A
ETM-B	Exhaust Gas Cleaning (EGC) System—Technical Manual for Scheme B
FCP	Fire Control Plan
GISIS	Global Integrated Ship Information System
GMDSS	Global Maritime Distress and Safety System
Grain Code	International Code for the Safe Carriage of Grain in Bulk
GRB	Garbage Record Book
HSC	High-speed craft
IAPP	International Air Pollution Prevention Certificate
IBC Code	International Code for the Construction and Equipment of Ships carrying Dangerous Chemicals in Bulk
IEE Certificate	International Energy Efficiency Certificate
IEEC	International Energy Efficiency Certificate
IG	Inert gas
IGC Code	International Code for the Construction and Equipment of Ships Carrying Liquefied Gases in Bulk 1988
ILO	International Labour Organisation
IMDG Code	International Code for the Maritime Transport of Dangerous Goods in Packaged Form
IMO	International Maritime Organisation
IMSBC	International Maritime Solid Bulk Cargoes Code
IOPP	International Oil Pollution Prevention Certificate
ISM	International Safety Management Code
ISPS	International Ship and Port Security
LL 1966	Load Lines Convention 1966
LL PROT 1988	Load Lines Protocol 1988
LRIT	Long-Range Identification and Tracking
LSA	Lifesaving appliances
MARPOL	International Convention for the Prevention of Pollution from Ships
MFAG	Medical First Aid Guide
MLC 2006	Maritime Labour Convention, 2006
MODU	Mobile Offshore Drilling Units
MSDS	Material Safety Data Sheets
MSMD	Minimum Safe Manning Document
NLS	Noxious Liquid Substance
NO_x	Nitrogen oxide

OMM	Onboard Management Manual
OOW	Officer of the Watch
ORB	Oil Record Book
P and A Manual	Procedures and Arrangements
PAH	Polycyclic aromatic hydrocarbons
pH	Potential of Hydrogen
PPM	Parts Per Million
PSC	Port State Control
PSCO	Port State Control Officer
RFPNW	Rating Forming Part of a Navigational Watch
RO	Recognised organisation
SEC	Safety Equipment Certificate
SECC	SO_x Emissions Compliance Certificate
SECP	SO_x Emissions Compliance Plan
SEEMP	Ship Energy Efficiency Management Plan
SMC	Safety Management Certificate
SMPEP	Shipboard Marine Pollution Emergency Plan
SMS	Safety Management System
SOC	Statement of Compliance
SOLAS 1974/78	International Convention for the Safety of Life at Sea
SOPEP	Shipboard Oil Pollution Emergency Plan
SO_x	Sulphur oxide
STCW	International Convention on Standards of Training, Certification and Watchkeeping for Seafarers
TDC	IMO Code of Safe Practice for Ships Carrying Timber Deck Cargoes
TONNAGE 1969	International Convention on Tonnage Measurement of Ships 1966
UHF	Ultra High Frequency
UTC	Coordinated Universal Time
VDR	Voyage data recorder
VHF	Very High Frequency
VOC	Volatile Organic Compounds

Port State Control Regime

1.1 Application and Scope

This book is intended to provide basic guidance on the responsibilities and conduct of Port State Control inspections in respect of the control provisions of relevant conventions and parts of the *IMO Instruments Implementation Code (III Code)* (resolution A.1070(28)) and afford consistency in the conduct of these inspections, the recognition of deficiencies of a vessel, its equipment, or its crew, and the application of control procedures. The Port State Control procedures apply to vessels which fall under the provision of the:

- International Convention for the Safety of Life at Sea, 1974, as amended (SOLAS 1974)
- Protocol of 1988 relating to the International Convention for the Safety of Life at Sea, 1974, as amended (SOLAS PROT 1988)
- International Convention on Load Lines, 1966, as amended (LL1966)
- Protocol of 1988 relating to the International Convention on Load Lines, 1966, as amended (LL PROT 1988)
- International Convention for the Prevention of Pollution from Ships, 1973, as modified by the 1978 and 1997 Protocols, as amended (MARPOL)
- International Convention on Standards of Training, Certification and Watchkeeping for Seafarers, 1978, as amended (STCW 1978)
- International Convention on Tonnage Measurement of Ships, 1969, as amended (TONNAGE 1969)
- International Convention on the Control of Harmful Anti-fouling Systems on Ships, 2001 (AFS 2001)
- Convention on the International Regulations for Preventing Collisions at Sea, 1972, as amended (COLREG 1972)

- International Convention on Civil Liability for Oil Pollution Damage, 1969 (CLC 1969)
- Protocol of 1992 to amend the International Convention on Civil Liability for Oil Pollution Damage, 1969, as amended (CLC PROT 1992)
- International Convention on Civil Liability for Bunker Oil Pollution Damage, 2001 (BUNKERS 2001)
- International Convention for the Control and Management of Ships' Ballast Water and Sediments, 2004, as amended (BWM 2004); and
- Nairobi International Convention on the Removal of Wrecks, 2007 (NAIROBI WRC 2007).

Vessels belonging to non-Parties should be afforded no more or less favourable treatment than for signatory Parties. For vessels below convention size, alternative provisions apply, which are discussed later. When exercising Port State Control, Parties should apply only those provisions of the conventions which are in force at that time, and which have been accepted. Where the provisions of a relevant convention are not specific, the Port State Control Officer should, in principle, apply the design arrangements as approved by the Flag State and, where appropriate, liaise with the Flag Administration. The Port State Control Officer should be aware that the provisions of relevant conventions permit Flag State Administrations to grant exceptions, allow equivalencies, and approve alternative design and arrangements (ADA). When an Exemption Certificate is issued in accordance with the relevant provisions of a convention, provided it includes the correct reference to the exemption documentation and the requirement to which it relates, or the vessel carries the approved ADA documentation (for example, SOLAS 1974 regulation II-1/55.4.2), port State authorities should interpret this as meaning that the vessel complies with the provisions of the convention. Port State Authorities should check, whenever possible, with the Flag State Administration should there be any doubt whether an exemption, equivalence or ADA has been granted. Notwithstanding the need to apply only those conventions which are currently in force, in relation to voluntary early implementation of amendments to SOLAS 1974 and related mandatory instruments, Parties should account for the *Guidelines on the voluntary early implementation of amendments to the 1974 SOLAS Convention and related mandatory instruments* (MSC.1/Circ.1565).

If a Port State exercises control based on the:

1. International Labour Organisation (ILO) Maritime Labour Convention, 2006, as amended (MLC 2006), guidance on the conduct of such inspections is given in the ILO publication *"Guidelines for port State control officers carrying out inspections under the Maritime Labour Convention, 2006, as amended"*; or
2. ILO Convention No.147, Merchant Shipping (Minimum Standards) Convention, 1976, or the Protocol of 1996 to the Merchant Shipping (Minimum Standards) Convention,

1976, guidance on the conduct of such inspections is given in the ILO publication *"Inspection of labour conditions on board ship: Guidelines for procedure"*.

Under the provisions of the relevant conventions set out above, the Administration (i.e. the Government of the Flag State) is responsible for promulgating laws and regulations and for taking all other steps which may be necessary to give the relevant conventions full and complete effect so to ensure that, from the point of view of safety of life and pollution prevention, a vessel is fit for the service for which it is intended and seafarers are qualified and fit for their duties. The nature of international shipping means that vessels may not frequently call at ports in their Flag State. It is therefore common for Flag States to appoint nominated surveyors at foreign ports and to authorise recognised organisations (ROs) to carry out inspection duties on the Flag State's behalf in accordance with the provisions of various conventions. The following control procedures should be regarded as complementary to national measures taken by Flag State Administrations in their countries and abroad and are intended to provide a common and consistent approach to the performance of Port State Control inspections and control measures taken because of the detection of serious deficiencies. The procedures set out herein are also intended to aid Flag State Administrations in ensuring compliance with convention provisions with respect to safeguarding the safety of crew, passengers and vessels, and ensuring the prevention of pollution of the marine and surrounding environments.

1.1.1 Provision for Port State Control

SOLAS 1974 regulations I/19, IX/6.2, XI-1/4 and XI-2/9, as modified by SOLAS PROT 1988; Article 21 of LL 1966, as modified by LL PROT 1988; Articles 5 and 6, regulation 11 of Annex I, regulation 16.9 of Annex II, regulation 9 of Annex III, regulation 14 of Annex IV, regulation 9 of Annex V and regulation 10 of Annex VI of MARPOL; Article X of STCW 1978; Article 12 of TONNAGE 1969, Article 11 of AFS 2001 and Article 9 of BWM 2004 provide for control procedures to be followed by a Party to a relevant convention with regard to foreign vessels visiting their ports. The authorities of Port States should make effective use of these provisions for the purposes of identifying deficiencies, if any, in such vessels which may render them substandard and for ensuring that remedial measures are taken.

1.1.2 Vessels of Non-parties

Article I(3) of SOLAS PROT 1988, Article I(3) of LL PROT 1988, Article 5(4) of MARPOL, Article X(5) of STCW 1978, Article 3(3) of AFS 2001 and Article 3(3) of BWM 2004 provides that no more favourable treatment may be given to the vessels of countries which are not Party to a relevant convention. All Parties should, as a matter of principle, apply the procedures to vessels of non-Parties to ensure that equivalent surveys and inspections are carried out and an equivalent level of safety and protection of the marine environment is ensured. As vessels of non-Parties are not provided with SOLAS, Load Lines, MARPOL, AFS or BWM certificates, as applicable, or the crew members may not hold STCW certificates, the Port State Control Officer, accounting for the principles established in the Port State Control Procedures, should be satisfied that the vessel and crew do not present a danger to those on board or an unreasonable threat of harm to the marine environment. If the vessel or crew has some form of certification other than that required by a convention, the Port State Control Officer may take the form and content of this documentation into account in the evaluation of that vessel. The conditions of and on such a vessel and its equipment and the certification of the crew and the Flag State's minimum manning standard should be compatible with the aims of the provisions of the conventions; otherwise, the vessel should be subject to such restrictions as are necessary to obtain a comparable level of safety and protection of the marine environment.

1.1.3 Vessels Below Conventional Size

In the exercise of their functions, Port State Control Officers should be guided by any certificates and other documents issued by or on behalf of the Flag State Administration. In such cases, the Port State Control Officer should limit the scope of inspection to the verification of compliance with those certificates and documents. To the extent a relevant instrument is not applicable to a vessel below convention size, the Port State Control Officer's task should be to assess whether the vessel is of an acceptable standard in respect to safety and the marine environment. In making that assessment, the Port State Control Officer should take due account of such factors as the length and nature of the intended voyage or service, the size and type of the vessel, the equipment provided and the nature of the cargo.

1.1.4 Professional Profile of Port State Control Officer

Port State Control should be carried out only by qualified Port State Control Officers who satisfy the minimum required qualifications and training. When the required professional expertise cannot be provided by the Port State Control Officer, the Port State Control Officer may be assisted by any person with the required expertise, as accepted by the Port State. Port State Control Officers and persons assisting them should be free from any commercial, financial and other pressures and have no commercial interest in the port of inspection, the vessels inspected, vessel repair facilities or any support services in the port or elsewhere, nor should Port State Control Officers be employed by or undertake work on behalf of ROs or classification societies. A Port State Control Officer should carry a personal document in the form of an identity card issued by the Port State and indicating that the Port State Control Officer is authorised to carry out the control.

1.1.5 Qualification and Training Requirements for Port State Control Officers

The Port State Control Officer should be an experienced officer qualified as Flag State surveyor. The Port State Control Officer should be able to communicate in English with key crew members and senior vessel's officers. Training should be provided for Port State Control Officers which imparts the necessary knowledge of the provisions of the relevant conventions that are relevant to the conduct of Port State Control, accounting for the latest *IMO Model Courses for Port State Control* officials. In specifying the qualifications and training requirements for Port State Control Officers, the Flag State Administration should account for, as appropriate, which of the internationally agreed instruments are relevant for control by the Port State and the types of vessels which may enter its ports. Port State Control Officers carrying out inspections of operational requirements should be qualified as a master or chief engineer and have appropriate seagoing experience, or have qualifications from an institution recognised by the Flag State Administration in a maritime-related field and have specialised training to ensure adequate competence and skill, or be a qualified officer of the Flag State Administration with an equivalent level of experience and training, for performing inspections of the relevant operational requirements. Port State Control Officers should attend periodic training sessions to update their knowledge with respect to instruments related to Port State Control duties and tasks.

1.2 Port State Inspections

In accordance with the provisions of the relevant conventions, signatory Parties may conduct inspections by Port State Control Officers of foreign vessels in their ports. Such inspections may be undertaken:

1. On the initiative of the signatory Party
2. At the request of, or based on information regarding a vessel provided by, another signatory Party; or
3. Based on information regarding a vessel provided by a member of the crew, a professional body, an association, a trade union or any other individual with an interest in the safety of the vessel, its crew and passengers, or the protection of the marine environment.

Whereas signatory Parties may entrust surveys and inspections of vessels entitled to fly their own Flag either to inspectors nominated for this purpose or to ROs, they should be aware that, under the relevant conventions, foreign vessels are subject to Port State Control, including boarding, inspection, remedial action and possible detention, only by officers duly authorised by the Port State. This authorisation of Port State Control Officers may be a general grant of authority or may be specific on a case-by-case basis. All possible efforts should be made to avoid a vessel being unduly detained or delayed. If a vessel is unduly detained or delayed, it should be entitled to compensation for any loss or damage suffered.

1.2.1 Initial Inspections

In the pursuance of control procedures under the relevant conventions, which, for instance, may arise from information given to a Port State regarding a vessel, a Port State Control Officer may proceed to the vessel and, before boarding, gain, from its appearance in the water, an impression of its standard of maintenance from such items as the condition of its paintwork, corrosion or pitting or unrepaired damage. At the earliest possible opportunity, the Port State Control Officer should ascertain the type of vessel, year of build and size of the vessel for the purpose of determining which provisions of the conventions are applicable. On boarding and introduction to the vessel's master or the responsible vessel's officer, the Port State Control Officer should examine the vessel's relevant certificates and documents required by the relevant conventions, as listed in appendix 12. In doing so, Port State Control Officers should note the following:

1. Certificates may be in hard copy or electronic form
2. Where the vessel relies upon electronic certificates:
   a. The certificates and website used to access them should conform with the *Guidelines for the use of electronic certificates* (FAL.5/Circ.39/Rev.2 and Corr.1)
   b. Specific verification instructions are to be available on the vessel; and
   c. Viewing such certificates on a computer is considered as meeting the requirement that certificates be "on board".
3. When examining International Tonnage Certificates, the Port State Control Officer should be guided by appendix 10; and
4. When examining certificates or documentary evidence of seafarers issued in accordance with STCW 1978, the Port State Control Officer should be guided by appendix 11; the list of certificates or documentary evidence required under STCW 1978 is also found in table B-I/2 of the STCW Code.

After the certificate and document inspection, the Port State Control Officer should check the overall condition of the vessel, including its equipment, navigational bridge, forecastle, cargo holds and cargo areas, engine room, and pilot transfer arrangements, and verify that any outstanding deficiency from the previous Port State Control inspection has been rectified. If the certificates required by the relevant conventions are valid and the Port State Control Officer's general impression and visual observations on board confirm a good standard of maintenance, the Port State Control Officer should generally confine the inspection to reported or observed deficiencies, if any. In pursuance of control procedures under chapter IX of SOLAS 1974 in relation to the International Safety Management Code (ISM Code), the Port State Control Officer should utilise the guidelines provided at appendix 8. If, however, the Port State Control Officer from general impressions or observations on board has clear grounds for believing that the vessel, its equipment or its crew do not substantially meet safety or competence requirements, the Port State Control Officer should proceed to a more detailed inspection. In forming such an impression, the Port State Control Officer should utilise the guidelines provided in the relevant appendices.

1.2.2 General Procedural Guidelines for Port State Control Officers

The Port State Control Officer should observe the *Code of good practice for Port State Control Officers* (MSC-MEPC.4/Circ.2), as provided at appendix 1, use professional judgement in carrying out their duties and consider consulting others as deemed appropriate. When boarding a vessel, the Port State Control Officer should present to the vessel's master, or to the representative of the owner, if requested to do so, the Port State Control Officer identification card. This card should be accepted as documented evidence that the Port State Control Officer in question is duly authorised by the Flag State Administration to carry out Port State Control inspections. If the Port State Control Officer has clear grounds for carrying out a more detailed inspection, the vessel's master should be immediately informed of these grounds and advised that, if so desired, the vessel's master may contact the Flag State Administration or, as appropriate, the RO responsible for issuing the certificate and invite their presence on board. In the event an inspection is initiated based on a report or complaint, especially where it is derived from a member of the vessel's crew, the source of the information should be treated in confidence and not be disclosed. When exercising control, all possible efforts should be made to avoid a vessel being unduly detained or delayed. It should be borne in mind that the main purpose of Port State Control is to prevent a substandard vessel from proceeding to sea. The Port State Control Officer should exercise professional judgement to determine whether to detain a vessel until the deficiencies are corrected or to allow it to sail with certain deficiencies, having due regard to the specific circumstances of the intended voyage. It should be recognised that all equipment is subject to failure and spares, or replacement parts may not be readily available. In such cases, undue delay should not be caused if, in the opinion of the Port State Control Officer, safe alternative arrangements have been made. Where the grounds for detention are the result of accidental damage suffered to a vessel, no detention order should be issued, provided that:

1. Due account has been given to the convention requirements regarding notification to the Flag State Administration, the nominated surveyor or the RO responsible for issuing the relevant certificate
2. Prior to entering a port, the vessel's master or company has submitted to the Port State Authority details of the circumstances of the accident and the damage suffered and information about the required notification of the Flag State Administration
3. Appropriate remedial action, to the satisfaction of the Port State Authority, is being taken by the vessel; and
4. The Port State Authority has ensured, having been notified of the completion of the remedial action, that deficiencies which were clearly hazardous to safety, health or environment have been rectified.

Since detention of a vessel is a serious matter involving many issues, it may be in the best interest of the Port State Control Officer to act together with other interested parties. For example, the Port State Control Officer may request the owner's representatives to provide proposals for correcting the situation. The Port State Control Officer should also consider cooperating with the Flag State Administration's representatives or the RO responsible for issuing the relevant certificates and consulting them regarding their acceptance of the owner's proposals and their possible additional requirements. Without limiting the Port State Control Officer's discretion in any way, the involvement of other parties could result in a safer vessel, avoid subsequent arguments relating to the circumstances of the detention and prove advantageous in the case of litigation involving "undue delay". Where deficiencies cannot be remedied at the port of inspection, the Port State Control Officer may allow the vessel to proceed to another port, subject to any appropriate conditions determined. In such circumstances, the Port State Control Officer should ensure that the competent authority of the next port of call and the Flag State are notified. Detention reports to the Flag State should be in sufficient detail for an assessment to be made of the severity of the deficiencies giving rise to the detention. The company or its representative have a right of appeal against a detention taken by the authority of a Port State. The appeal should not cause the detention to be suspended. The Port State Control Officer should properly inform the vessel's master of the right of appeal. To ensure consistent enforcement of Port State Control requirements, Port State Control Officers are advised to carry an extract of the *General procedural guidelines for Port State Control Officers* for ready reference when carrying out any Port State Control inspections.

1.2 Port State Inspections

1.2.3 Clear Grounds

When a Port State Control Officer inspects a foreign vessel which is required to hold a convention certificate and which is in a port or an offshore terminal under the jurisdiction of the Port State, any such inspection should be limited to verifying that there are on board valid certificates and other relevant documentation and the Port State Control Officer forming an impression of the overall condition of the vessel, its equipment and its crew, unless there are "clear grounds" for believing that the condition of the vessel or its equipment does not correspond substantially with the particulars of the certificates. "Clear grounds" to conduct a more detailed inspection include but are not limited to:

1. The absence of principal equipment or arrangements required by the relevant conventions
2. Evidence from a review of the vessel's certificates that a certificate or certificates are invalid
3. Evidence that certificates and documents required by the relevant conventions and listed in appendix 12, part A, are not on board, incomplete, not maintained or are falsely maintained
4. Evidence from the Port State Control Officer's general impressions and observations that serious hull or structural deterioration or deficiencies exist that may place at risk the structural, watertight or weathertight integrity of the vessel
5. Evidence from the Port State Control Officer's general impressions or observations that serious deficiencies exist in the safety, pollution prevention or navigational equipment
6. Information or evidence that the vessel's master or crew are not familiar with essential shipboard operations relating to the safety of vessels or the prevention of pollution, or that such operations have not been carried out
7. Indications that key crew members may not be able to communicate with each other or with other persons on board
8. The emission of false distress alerts not followed by proper cancellation procedures; and
9. Receipt of a report or complaint containing information that a vessel appears to be substandard.

1.2.4 More Detailed Inspections

If the vessel does not carry valid certificates, or if the Port State Control Officer, from general impressions or observations on board, has clear grounds for believing that the condition of the vessel or its equipment does not correspond substantially with the particulars of the certificates or that the vessel's master or crew is not familiar with essential shipboard procedures, a more detailed inspection, as described in this chapter, should be carried out, utilising the guidance provided in the relevant appendices. Support during the more detailed inspection may be found in the documents mentioned in appendix 12, part B, where applicable. It is not envisaged that all the equipment and procedures outlined in this chapter would be checked during a single Port State Control inspection unless the condition of the vessel or the familiarity of the vessel's master or crew with essential shipboard procedures necessitates such a detailed inspection. In addition, these procedures are not intended to impose the seafarer certification programme of the Port State on a vessel entitled to fly the Flag of another signatory Party to STCW 1978 or to impose control procedures on foreign vessels more than those imposed on vessels of the Port State.

1.3 Contravention and Detention

1.3.1 Identification of a Substandard Vessel

In general, a vessel may be regarded as substandard if the hull, machinery, equipment or operational safety and the protection of the environment is substantially below the standards required by the relevant conventions or if the crew are not in conformity with the safe manning document, owing to, inter alia:

1. The absence of principal equipment or arrangement required by the conventions
2. Non-compliance of equipment or arrangement with relevant specifications of the conventions
3. Substantial deterioration of the vessel or its equipment
4. Insufficiency of operational proficiency, or unfamiliarity with essential operational procedures by the crew; and
5. Insufficiency of manning or insufficiency of certification of seafarers.

If these evident factors as a whole or individually pose a danger to the vessel or persons on board or present an unreasonable threat of harm to the marine environment if it were allowed to proceed to sea, it should be regarded as a substandard vessel. The Port State Control Officer should also account for the guidelines provided at Chap. 3.

1.3.2 Submission of Information Concerning Deficiencies

Information that a vessel appears to be substandard could be submitted to the appropriate authorities of the Port State by a member of the crew, a professional body, an association, a trade union or any other individual with an interest in the safety of the vessel, its crew and passengers, or the protection of the marine environment. This information should be submitted in writing to permit proper documentation of the case and of the alleged deficiencies. If the information is passed verbally, the filing of a written report should be required, identifying, for the purposes of the Port State's records, the individual or body providing the information. The attending Port State Control Officer may collect this information and submit it as part of the Port State Control Officer's report if the originator is unable to do so. Information which may cause an investigation should be submitted as early as possible, giving adequate time to the authorities to act as necessary. Each Party to the relevant convention should determine which authorities should receive information on substandard vessels and initiate action. Measures should be taken to ensure that information submitted to the wrong department is promptly passed on by such department to the appropriate authority for action.

1.3.3 Port State Action in Response to Alleged Substandard Vessels

On receipt of information about an alleged substandard vessel or alleged pollution risk, the authorities should immediately investigate the matter and take the action required by the circumstances in accordance with the preceding sections. Authorities which receive information about a substandard vessel that could give rise to detention should forthwith notify any maritime, consular and or diplomatic representatives of the Flag State in the area of the vessel and request them to initiate or cooperate with investigations. Likewise, the RO which has issued the relevant certificates on behalf of the Flag State should be notified. These provisions will not, however, relieve the authorities of the Port State, being a Party to a relevant convention, of the responsibility for taking appropriate action in accordance with its powers under the relevant conventions. If the Port State receiving information is unable to act because there is insufficient time or no Port State Control Officers can be made available before the vessel sails, the information should be passed to the authorities of the country of the next appropriate port of call, to the Flag State and to the RO in that port, where appropriate.

1.3.4 Responsibilities of Port State to Take Remedial Action

If a Port State Control Officer determines that a vessel can be regarded as substandard as specified above and in accordance with appendix 2, the Port State should immediately ensure that corrective action is taken to safeguard the safety of the vessel and passengers and or crew and eliminate any threat of harm to the marine environment before permitting the vessel to sail.

1.3.5 Guidance for the Detention of Vessels

Notwithstanding the fact that it is impracticable to define a vessel as substandard solely by reference to a list of qualifying defects, guidance for the detention of vessels is given at appendix 2.

1.3.6 Suspension of Inspection

In exceptional circumstances where, resulting from a more detailed inspection, the overall condition of a vessel and its equipment, also accounting for the crew conditions, is found to be obviously substandard, the Port State Control Officer may suspend an inspection. Prior to suspending an inspection, the Port State Control Officer should have recorded detainable deficiencies in the areas set out at appendix 2, as appropriate. The suspension of the inspection may continue until the responsible parties have taken the steps necessary to ensure that the vessel complies with the requirements of the relevant instruments. In cases where the vessel is detained and an inspection is suspended, the Port State Authority should notify the responsible parties without delay. The notification should include information about the detention, and state that the inspection is suspended until that authority has been informed that the vessel complies with all relevant requirements.

1.3.7 Procedures for Rectification of Deficiencies and Release

The Port State Control Officer should endeavour to secure the rectification of all deficiencies detected. In the case of deficiencies which are clearly hazardous to safety or the environment, the Port State Control Officer should, except as provided in the paragraph below, ensure that the hazard is removed before the vessel is allowed to proceed to sea. For this purpose, appropriate action should be taken, which may include detention or a formal prohibition of a vessel to continue an operation due to established deficiencies which, individually or together, would render the continued operation hazardous.

Where deficiencies which caused a detention, as referred to in the paragraph above, cannot be remedied in the port of inspection, the Port State Authority may allow the vessel concerned to proceed to the nearest appropriate repair yard available, as chosen by the vessel's master and agreed to by that authority, provided that the conditions agreed between the Port State Authority and the Flag State are complied with. Such conditions will ensure that the vessel should not sail until it can proceed without risk to the safety of the passengers or crew, or risk to other vessels, or without presenting an unreasonable threat of harm to the marine environment. Such conditions may include confirmation from the Flag State that remedial action has been taken on the vessel in question. In such circumstances the Port State Authority should notify the authority of the vessel's next port of call, the parties mentioned in Chap. 4 and any other authority as appropriate. Notification to authorities should be made in the form shown at appendix 14. The authority receiving such notification should inform the notifying authority of action taken and may use the form shown at appendix 15. On the condition that all possible efforts have been made to rectify all other deficiencies, except those referred to in below, the vessel may be allowed to proceed to a port where any such deficiencies can be rectified. If a vessel proceeds to sea without complying with the conditions agreed to by the authority of the port of inspection, that Port State authority should immediately alert the next port, if known, the Flag State and all other authorities it considers appropriate. If a vessel does not call at the nominated repair port, the Port State Authority of the repair port should immediately alert the Flag State and detaining Port State, which may take appropriate action, and notify any other authority it considers appropriate.

1.4 Reporting and Review Requirements

1.4.1 Port State Reporting

Port State authorities should ensure that, at the conclusion of an inspection, the master of the vessel is provided with a document showing the results of the inspection, details of any action taken by the Port State Control Officer, and a list of any corrective action to be initiated by the vessel's master and or company. Such reports should be made in accordance with the format provided at annex B. Where, in the exercise of Port State Control, a Party denies a foreign vessel entry to the ports or offshore terminals under its jurisdiction, whether resulting from information about a substandard vessel or not, it should forthwith provide the vessel's master and Flag State with reasons for the denial of entry. In the case of a detention, at least an initial notification should be made to the Flag State Administration as soon as practicable. If such notification is made verbally, it should be subsequently confirmed in writing. As a minimum, the notification should include details of the vessel's name, the IMO number, copies of Forms A and B as set out at annexes B and C, time of detention and copies of any detention order. Likewise, the ROs which have issued the relevant certificates on behalf of the Flag State should be notified, where appropriate. The parties above should also be notified in writing of the release of detention. As a minimum, this information should include the vessel's name, the IMO number, the date and time of release and a copy of Form B as set out at annex C. If the vessel has been allowed to sail with known deficiencies, the authorities of the Port State should communicate all the facts to the authorities of the country of the next appropriate port of call, to the Flag State, and to the RO, where appropriate.

Parties to a relevant convention, when they have exercised control giving rise to detention, should submit to the IMO reports in accordance with SOLAS 1974 regulation I/19, Article 11 of MARPOL, or Article X(3) of STCW 1978. Such deficiency reports should be made in accordance with the form provided at appendices 13 or 16, as appropriate, or may be submitted electronically by the Port State or a regional Port State Control regime. Copies of such deficiency reports should, in addition to being forwarded to the IMO, be sent by the Port State without delay to the authorities of the Flag State and, where appropriate, to the RO which had issued the relevant certificate. Deficiencies found which are not related to the relevant conventions, or which involve vessels of non-Parties or below convention size, should be submitted to Flag States and or to appropriate organisations but not to the IMO. Relevant telephone numbers and addresses of Flag States' headquarters to which reports should be sent as outlined above, as well as addresses of Flag State offices which provide inspection services should be provided to the IMO.[1]

1.4.2 Flag State Reporting

On receiving a report on detention, the Flag State and, where appropriate, the RO through the Flag State Administration, should, as soon as possible, inform the IMO of remedial action taken in respect of the detention, which may be submitted electronically by the Flag State to the Global Integrated Ship Information System (GISIS) or in a format shown at appendix 17. Relevant telephone numbers and addresses of Port State Control offices, headquarters and those who provide inspection services should be provided to the IMO.

1.4.3 Reporting of Allegations Under MARPOL

A report on alleged deficiencies or on alleged contravention of the discharge provisions relating to the provisions of MARPOL should be forwarded to the Flag State as soon as possible, preferably no later than 60 days after the observation of the deficiencies or contravention. Such reports may be made in accordance with the format provided at appendices 13 or 16, as appropriate. If a contravention of the discharge provisions is suspected, then the information should be supplemented by evidence of violations which, as a minimum, should include the information specified in parts 2 and 3 of appendices 3 and 4. On receiving a report on alleged deficiencies or alleged contravention of the discharge provisions, the Flag State and, where appropriate, the RO through the Flag State Administration, should, as soon as possible, inform the Party submitting the report of immediate action taken in respect of the alleged deficiencies or contravention. That Party and the IMO should, upon completion of such action, be informed of the outcome and details, where appropriate, be included in the mandatory annual report to the IMO.

---

[1] Such addresses are available in MSC-MEPC.6/Circ.19 (National contact points for safety and pollution prevention and response), which may be amended, the IMO Internet home page and the GISIS module on contact points (http://gisis.imo.org/Public).

1.5 Review Procedures

In the interest of making information regarding deficiencies and remedial measures generally available, a summary of such reports should be made by the IMO in a timely manner in order that the information can be disseminated in accordance with the IMO's procedures to all Parties to the relevant conventions. In the summary of deficiency reports, an indication should be given of Flag State action or whether a comment by the Flag State concerned is outstanding. The appropriate committee should periodically evaluate the summary of the deficiency reports to identify measures that may be necessary to ensure more consistent and effective application of IMO instruments, paying close attention to the difficulties reported by Parties to the relevant conventions, particularly in respect of developing countries in their capacity as Port States. Recommendations to address such difficulties, when recognised by the appropriate committee, should, where appropriate, be incorporated into the relevant IMO instrument and any modifications relating to the procedures and obligations should be made in the Port State documentation.

Conduct of Port State Control Officers

This book is adapted from IMO Resolution A.1155(32) within the framework of the regional memoranda of understanding and agreement on Port State Control (MSC-MEPC.4/CIRC.2). The Code provides guidelines regarding the standards of integrity, professionalism and transparency that regional Port State Control regimes expect of all Port State Control Officers who are involved in or associated with Port State Control inspections. The objective of the Code is to assist Port State Control Officers in conducting their inspections to the highest professional level. Port State Control Officers are central to achieving the aims of the regional Port State Control regime. They are the daily contact with the shipping world, and as such, are expected to act within the law, within the rules of their Government and in a fair, open, impartial and consistent manner. The Code encompasses three fundamental principles against which all actions of Port State Control Officers are judged: integrity, professionalism and transparency. These are defined as follows:

1. *Integrity* is the state of moral soundness, honesty and freedom from corrupting influences or motives;
2. *Professionalism* is applying accepted professional standards of conduct and technical knowledge. For Port State Control Officers, standards of behaviour are established by the maritime authority and the general consent of the Port State members; and
3. *Transparency* implies openness and accountability.

The list of the actions and behaviour expected of Port State Control Officers in applying these principles is set out in the section below. Adhering to professional standards provides greater credibility to Port State Control Officers and places more significance on their findings. Nothing in the Code may absolve Port State Control Officers from complying with the specific requirements of the Port State Control instruments and applicable national laws.

2.1 Conduct of Port State Control Officers

2.1.1 Actions and Behaviours Expected of Port State Control Officers

Port State Control Officers are expected to:

- Use their professional judgement in carrying out their duties.

2.1.1.1 Respect

- Remember that a vessel is a home as well as a workplace for the vessel's personnel and not unduly disturb their rest or privacy
- Comply with any vessel housekeeping rules such as removing dirty shoes or work clothes
- Not be prejudiced by the race, gender, religion or nationality of the crew when making decisions and treat all personnel on board with respect
- Respect the authority of the vessel's master or their deputy
- Be polite but professional and firm as required
- Never become threatening, abrasive or dictatorial or use language that may cause offence
- Expect to be treated with courtesy and respect.

2.1.1.2 Conduct of Inspections

- Comply with all health and safety requirements of the vessel and their Administration, for example, wearing of personal protective clothing, and not take any action or cause any action to be taken which could compromise the safety of the Port State Control Officer or the vessel's crew
- Comply with all security requirements of the vessel and wait to be escorted around the vessel by a responsible person
- Present their identification cards to the vessel's master or the representative of the owner at the start of the inspection

- Explain the reason for the inspections; however, where the inspection is triggered by a report or complaint, they must not reveal the identity of the person making the complaint
- Apply the procedures of Port State Control and the convention requirements in a consistent and professional way and interpret them pragmatically when necessary
- Not try to mislead the crew, for example by asking them to do things that are contrary to the relevant conventions
- Request the crew to demonstrate the functioning of equipment and operational activities, such as drills, and not make tests themselves
- Seek advice when they are unsure of a requirement or of their findings rather than making an uninformed decision, for example by consulting colleagues, publications, the Flag Administration, the recognised organisation
- Where it is safe to do so accommodate the operational needs of the port and the vessel
- Explain clearly to the vessel's master the findings of the inspection and the corrective action required and ensure that the report of inspection is clearly understood
- Issue to the vessel's master a legible and comprehensible report of inspection before leaving the vessel.

2.1.1.3 Disagreements

- Deal with any disagreement over the conduct or findings of the inspection calmly and patiently
- Advise the vessel's master of the complaints procedure in place if the disagreement cannot be resolved within a reasonable time
- Advise the vessel's master of the right of appeal and relevant procedures in the case of detention.

2.1.1.4 Integrity

- Be independent and not have any commercial interest in their ports and the vessels they inspect or companies providing services in their ports. For example, Port State Control Officers should not be employed, even on an occasional basis, by companies which operate vessels in their ports or Port State Control Officers should not have an interest in the repair companies in their ports
- Be free to make decisions based on the findings of their inspections and not on any commercial considerations of the port
- Always follow the rules of their Administrations regarding the acceptance of gifts and favours, for example, meals on board

- Firmly refuse any attempts of bribery and report any blatant cases to the maritime authority
- Not misuse their authority for benefit, financial or otherwise.

2.1.1.5 Updating Knowledge

- Update their technical knowledge regularly.

Detention of Vessels

3

In taking a decision concerning the rectification of a deficiency or detention of a vessel, the Port State Control Officer will have to take into consideration the results of the more detailed inspection. The Port State Control Officer will exercise professional judgement in determining whether to detain the vessel until the deficiencies are rectified or to allow the vessel to sail with certain deficiencies without unreasonable danger to safety, health or the environment, having also considered the specific circumstances of the intended voyage.

3.1 Principles Governing Rectification of Deficiencies or Detention of a Vessel

3.1.1 Detention Related to Minimum Safe Manning and STCW Certification

Before detaining a vessel for the reasons of not operating at appropriate established minimum safe manning and STCW certification, the following will have to be considered, giving due regard to the points listed under areas under STCW 1978:

1. Length and nature of the intended voyage or service
2. Whether or not the deficiency poses a danger to vessels, persons on board or the environment
3. Whether or not appropriate hours of rest for the crew have been recorded and there is evidence that the minimum hours of rest have repeatedly not been kept
4. The vessel's size and type and equipment provided; and
5. The nature of cargo.

© The Author(s), under exclusive license to Springer Nature Switzerland AG 2025
A. A. Olsen and F. Karkori, *Ship's Officer's Guide to Port State Control*,
Synthesis Lectures on Ocean Systems Engineering,
https://doi.org/10.1007/978-3-031-77502-4_3

3.1.2 Procedures for the Detention of Vessels of All Sizes

When exercising professional judgement as to whether a vessel should be detained, the Port State Control Officer will apply the following criteria:

1. *Timing*: vessels which are unsafe to proceed to sea will be detained upon the first inspection, irrespective of the time the vessel will stay in port; and
2. *Re-inspection criterion*: the vessel will be detained if the deficiencies on a vessel are sufficiently serious to merit a Port State Control Officer returning to the vessel to be satisfied that they have been rectified before the vessel sails.

The need for the Port State Control Officer to return to the vessel classifies the seriousness of the deficiencies. When deciding whether the deficiencies found in a vessel are sufficiently serious to merit detention, the Port State Control Officer should assess whether:

1. The vessel has relevant, valid documentation; and
2. The vessel has the crew required in the minimum safe manning document or equivalent.

During inspection, the Port State Control Officer should further assess whether the vessel and or crew, throughout its forthcoming voyage, is able to:

1. Navigate safely
2. Safely handle, carry and monitor the condition of the cargo
3. Operate the engine room safely
4. Maintain proper propulsion and steering
5. Fight fires effectively in any part of the vessel if necessary
6. Abandon vessel speedily and safely and effect rescue if necessary
7. Prevent pollution of the environment
8. Maintain adequate stability
9. Maintain adequate watertight integrity
10. Communicate in distress situations if necessary; and
11. Provide safe and healthy conditions on board.

If the result of any of these assessments is negative, taking account of all deficiencies found, the vessel should be strongly considered for detention. A combination of deficiencies of a less serious nature may also warrant the detention of the vessel.

3.1.3 Invalid Certificates

The lack of valid certificates as required by the relevant conventions may warrant the detention of vessels. However, vessels flying the Flag of States not a Party to a convention or not having implemented another relevant instrument are not entitled to carry the certificates provided for by the convention or other relevant instrument. Therefore, absence of the required certificates should not by itself constitute a reason to detain these vessels; however, in applying the "no more favourable treatment" clause, substantial compliance with the provisions and criteria specified in the Port State Control Procedures must be required before the vessel sails.

3.1.4 Detainable Deficiencies

To assist the Port State Control Officer in the application of the Port State Control procedures, a list of deficiencies, grouped under relevant conventions and or codes, which may be considered of such a serious nature that they may warrant the detention of the vessel involved, are provided below. This list is not considered exhaustive but is intended to give examples of relevant items. However, the detainable deficiencies under STCW 1978, as listed below, are the only grounds for detention under this Convention.

3.1.4.1 Areas Under SOLAS 1974

1. Failure of proper operation of propulsion and other essential machinery, as well as electrical installations
2. Insufficient cleanliness of engine room, excess amount of oily-water mixture in bilges, insulation of piping including exhaust pipes in engine room contaminated by oil, and improper operation of bilge pumping arrangements
3. Failure of the proper operation of emergency generator, lighting, batteries and switches
4. Failure of proper operation of the main and auxiliary steering gear
5. Absence, failure, insufficient capacity or serious deterioration of personal life-saving appliances, survival craft and launching and recovery arrangements (see also MSC.1/Circ.1490/Rev.1)
6. Absence, non-compliance or substantial deterioration to the extent that it cannot comply with its intended use of fire detection system, fire alarms, firefighting equipment, fixed fire extinguishing installation, ventilation valves, fire dampers and quick-closing devices

7. Absence, substantial deterioration or failure of proper operation of the cargo deck area fire protection on tankers
8. Absence, non-compliance or serious deterioration of lights, shapes or sound signals
9. Absence or failure of the proper operation of the radio equipment for distress and safety communication
10. Absence or failure of the proper operation of navigation equipment, taking the relevant provisions of SOLAS 1974 regulation V/16.2 into account
11. Absence of corrected navigational charts, and or all other relevant nautical publications necessary for the intended voyage, taking account that electronic charts may be used as a substitute for the charts
12. Absence of non-sparking exhaust ventilation for cargo pump rooms
13. Serious deficiency in the operational requirements listed in appendix 7
14. Number, composition or certification of crew not corresponding with safe manning document
15. Non-implementation or failure to carry out the enhanced survey programme in accordance with SOLAS 1974 regulation XI-1/2 and the International Code on the Enhanced Programme of Inspections during Surveys of Bulk Carriers and Oil Tankers, 2011 (2011 ESP Code), as amended; and or
16. Absence or failure of a voyage data recorder (VDR) when its use is compulsory.

3.1.4.2 Areas Under the IBC Code

1. Transport of a substance not mentioned in the Certificate of Fitness or missing cargo information
2. Missing or damaged high-pressure safety devices
3. Electrical installations not intrinsically safe or not corresponding to the Code requirements
4. Sources of ignition in hazardous locations
5. Contravention of special requirements
6. Exceeding of maximum allowable cargo quantity per tank
7. Insufficient heat protection for sensitive products
8. Pressure alarms for cargo tanks not operable; and or
9. Transport of substances to be inhibited without valid inhibitor certificate.

3.1.4.3 Areas Under the IGC Code

1. Transport of a substance not mentioned in the Certificate of Fitness or missing cargo information
2. Missing closing devices for accommodations or service spaces
3. Bulkhead not gastight

4. Defective air locks
5. Missing or defective quick-closing valves
6. Missing or defective safety valves
7. Electrical installations not intrinsically safe or not corresponding to the IGC Code requirements
8. Ventilators in cargo area not operable
9. Pressure alarms for cargo tanks not operable
10. Gas detection plant and or toxic gas detection plant defective; and or
11. Transport of substances to be inhibited without valid inhibitor certificate.

3.1.4.4 Areas Under LL 1966 and LL PROT 1988

1. Significant areas of damage or corrosion or pitting of plating and associated stiffening in decks and hull affecting seaworthiness or strength to take local loads, unless properly authorised temporary repairs for a voyage to a port for permanent repairs have been carried out
2. A recognised case of insufficient stability
3. The absence of sufficient and reliable information, in an approved form, which by rapid and simple means enables the vessel's master to arrange for the loading and ballasting of the vessel in such a way that a safe margin of stability is maintained at all stages and at varying conditions of the voyage, and that the creation of any unacceptable stresses in the vessel's structure is avoided
4. Absence, substantial deterioration or defective closing devices, hatch closing arrangements and watertight/weathertight doors
5. Overloading
6. Absence of, or impossibility to read, draught marks and or Load Line Marks; and or
7. The means of freeing water from the deck not in satisfactory or operational condition.

3.1.4.5 Areas Under MARPOL Annex I

1. Absence, serious deterioration or failure of proper operation of the oily-water filtering equipment, the oil discharge monitoring and control system or the 15 ppm alarm arrangements
2. Remaining capacity of slop and or sludge tank insufficient for the intended voyage
3. Oil Record Book (ORB) not available
4. Unauthorised discharge bypass fitted
5. Failure to meet the requirements of regulation 20.4 or alternative requirements specified in regulation 20.7; and or
6. Oily bilge water and or oil residue accumulated in machinery spaces.

3.1.4.6 Areas Under MARPOL Annex II

1. Absence of Procedures and Arrangements Manual (P and A Manual)
2. Cargo is not categorised
3. No Cargo Record Book available; and or
4. Unauthorised discharge bypass fitted.

3.1.4.7 Areas Under MARPOL Annex III and Dangerous Goods Carriage Requirements

1. Absence of a valid Document of Compliance (DOC) for carriage of dangerous goods (if required)
2. Absence of a Dangerous Cargo Manifest or detailed stowage plan before departure of the vessel
3. Stowage and segregation provisions of the IMDG Code Sects. 7.1, 7.2, 7.4, 7.5 and 7.6 are not met
4. Vessel is carrying dangerous goods not in compliance with the DOC for carriage of dangerous goods of the vessel
5. Vessel is carrying damaged or leaking dangerous goods packages; and or
6. The vessel's personnel assigned to specific duties related to the cargo are not familiar with those duties, any dangers posed by the cargo and with the measures to be taken in such a context.

3.1.4.8 Areas Under MARPOL Annex IV

1. Absence of valid International Sewage Pollution Prevention Certificate
2. Sewage treatment plant not approved and certified by the Administration
3. Failure of sewage treatment plant; and or
4. Vessel's personnel not familiar with disposal/discharge requirements of sewage.

3.1.4.9 Areas Under MARPOL Annex V

1. Absence of garbage management plan
2. No garbage record book available; and or
3. Vessel's personnel not familiar with disposal/discharge requirements of garbage management plan.

3.1.4.10 Areas Under MARPOL Annex VI

1. Absence of valid International Air Pollution Prevention Certificate (IAPP Certificate) and where relevant Engine International Air Pollution Prevention Certificates (EIAPP Certificates) and Technical Files
2. A marine diesel engine with a power output of more than 130 kW which is installed on board a vessel constructed on or after 1 January 2000, or a marine diesel engine having undergone a major conversion on or after 1 January 2000 which does not comply with the NOx Technical Code 2008, as amended
3. The sulphur content of any fuel oil used on board vessels exceeds the limit of 0.5% m/m on and after 1 January 2020
4. The sulphur content of any fuel used on board exceeds 0.1% m/m while operating within a SOX emission control area as per the provisions of regulation 14
5. Emission reduction by equivalent arrangements is not met
6. An incinerator installed on board the vessel on or after 1 January 2000 does not comply with requirements contained in appendix IV to the annex, or the standard specifications for shipboard incinerators developed by the IMO (resolution MEPC.244(66))
7. Vessel's personnel are not familiar with essential procedures regarding the operation of air pollution prevention equipment
8. Absence of valid IEEC (International Energy Efficiency Certificate); and or
9. Absence of a Statement of Compliance (SOC) related to fuel oil consumption reporting on board.

3.1.4.11 Areas Under STCW 1978

1. Failure of seafarers to hold a certificate, to have an appropriate certificate, to have a valid dispensation or to provide documentary proof that an application for an endorsement has been submitted to the Administration
2. Failure to comply with the applicable safe manning requirements of the Administration
3. Failure of navigational or engineering watch arrangements to conform to the requirements specified for the vessel by the Administration
4. Absence in a watch of a person qualified to operate equipment essential to safe navigation, safety radiocommunications or the prevention of marine pollution; and or
5. Inability to provide for the first watch at the commencement of a voyage and for subsequent relieving watches persons who are sufficiently rested and otherwise fit for duty.

3.1.4.12 Areas Under AFS 2001

1. Absence of a valid International Anti-Fouling System Certificate or a Declaration on Anti-Fouling System; and or
2. Sampling proves it is non-compliant within the port's jurisdiction.

3.1.5 Areas Which May not Warrant a Detention, but Where, for Example, Cargo Operations Should be Suspended

Failure of the proper operation (or maintenance) of inert gas systems, cargo-related gear or machinery should be considered sufficient grounds to stop cargo operation.

Conduct of Investigations and Inspections Under MARPOL Annex I

4.1 Inspection of the IOPP Certificate, Vessel and Equipment

4.1.1 Vessels Required to Carry an IOPP Certificate

On boarding and introduction to the vessel's master or the responsible vessel's officer, the Port State Control Officer should examine the International Oil Pollution Prevention Certificate (IOPP Certificate), including the attached Supplement (Record of Construction and Equipment for (vessels other than) oil tankers) and the Oil Record Book. The Oil Record Book may be presented in an electronic format. A declaration from the Administration should be viewed to accept this electronic record book. If a declaration cannot be provided, a hard copy record book will need to be presented for examination. The certificate carries the information on the type of vessel and the dates of surveys and inspections. As a preliminary check it should be confirmed that the dates of surveys and inspections are still valid. Furthermore, it should be established if the vessel carries an oil cargo and whether the carriage of such oil cargo is in conformity with the certificate (refer also to para 1.11 of the *Record of Construction and Equipment for Oil Tankers*). Through examining the Record of Construction and Equipment, the Port State Control Officer may establish how the vessel is equipped for the prevention of marine pollution. If the certificate is valid and the general impression and visual observations on board confirm a good standard of maintenance, the Port State Control Officer should generally confine the inspection to reported deficiencies, if any. If, however, the Port State Control Officer from general impressions or observations on board has clear grounds for believing that the condition of the vessel or its equipment does not correspond substantially with the particulars of the certificate, a more detailed inspection should be initiated.

The inspection of the engine room should begin with forming a general impression of the state of the engine room, the presence of traces of oil in the engine room bilges and the vessel's routine for disposing of oil-contaminated water from the engine room spaces. Next, a closer examination of the vessel's equipment as listed in the IOPP Certificate may take place. This examination should also confirm that no unapproved modifications have been made to the vessel and its equipment. Should any doubt arise as to the maintenance or the condition of the vessel or its equipment, then further examination and testing may be conducted as considered necessary. In this respect reference is made to annex 3 to the *Survey Guidelines under the Harmonised System of Survey and Certification* (HSSC), 2021 (resolution A.1156(32)), as may be amended. The Port State Control Officer should bear in mind that a vessel may be equipped over and above the requirements of MARPOL Annex I. If such equipment is malfunctioning, the Flag State should be informed. This alone however should not cause a vessel to be detained unless the discrepancy presents an unreasonable threat of harm to the marine environment. In respect of oil tankers, the inspection should include the cargo tank and pump room area of the vessel and should begin with forming a general impression of the layout of the tanks, the cargoes carried, and the routine of cargo slops disposal.

4.1.2 Vessels of Non-parties to MARPOL Annex I and Other Vessels not Required to Carry an IOPP Certificate

As this category of vessels is not provided with an IOPP Certificate, the Port State Control Officer should be satisfied with respect to the construction and equipment standards relevant to the vessel based on the requirements set out in MARPOL Annex I. In all other respects the Port State Control Officer should be guided by the procedures for vessels referred to above. If the vessel has some form of certification other than the IOPP Certificate, the Port State Control Officer may take the form and content of this documentation into account in the evaluation of that vessel.

4.1.3 Control

In exercising the control functions, the Port State Control Officer should use professional judgement to determine whether to detain the vessel until any noted deficiencies are corrected or to allow it to sail with certain deficiencies which do not pose an unreasonable threat of harm to the marine environment. In doing this, the Port State Control Officer should be guided by the principle that the requirements contained in MARPOL Annex I, in respect of construction and equipment and the operation of vessels, are essential for the protection of the marine environment and that departure from these requirements could constitute an unreasonable threat of harm to the marine environment.

4.2 Contravention of the Discharge Provisions

Experience has shown that information furnished to the Flag State as envisaged in appendix 5 of this book is often inadequate to enable the Flag State to cause proceedings to be brought in respect of the alleged violation of the discharge requirements. This section is intended to identify information which is often needed by a Flag State for the prosecution of such possible violations. It is recommended that, in preparing a Port State report on deficiencies, where contravention of the discharge requirements is involved, the authorities of the coastal or Port State be guided by the itemised list of possible evidence as provided in this chapter. It should be borne in mind in this connection that:

1. the report aims to provide the optimal collation of obtainable data; however, even if all the information cannot be provided, as much information as possible should be submitted; and
2. it is important for all the information included in the report to be supported by facts which, when considered as a whole, would lead the Port or Coastal State to believe a contravention had occurred.

In addition to the Port State report on deficiencies, a report should be completed by a Port or Coastal State based on the itemised list of possible evidence. It is important that these reports are supplemented by documents such as:

1. A statement by the observer of the pollution; in addition to the information required under section 1 of part 3 of this chapter, the statement should include considerations which lead the observer to conclude that none of any other possible pollution sources is in fact the source
2. Statements concerning the sampling procedures both slick and on board; these should include location where and time when samples were taken, identity of person(s) taking the samples and receipts identifying the persons having custody and receiving transfer of the samples
3. Reports of analyses of samples taken of the slick and on board; the reports should include the results of the analyses, a description of the method employed, reference to or copies of scientific documentation attesting to the accuracy and validity of the method employed, and names of persons performing the analyses and their experience
4. A statement by the Port State Control Officer on board together with their rank and organisation
5. Statements by persons being questioned

6. Statements by witnesses; all observations, photographs and documentation should be supported by a signed verification of their authenticity; all certifications, authentications or verifications shall be executed in accordance with the laws of the State which prepares them; all statements should be signed and dated by the person making the statement and, if possible, by a witness to the signing; the names of the persons signing statements should be printed in legible script above or below the signature
7. Photographs of the oil slick; and
8. Copies or printouts of relevant recordings, etc., pages of the oil record book, logbooks, discharge.

The report should be sent to the Flag State. If the Coastal State observing the pollution and the Port State carrying out the investigation on board are not the same, the State carrying out the latter investigation should also send a copy of its findings to the State observing the pollution and requesting the investigation.

4.3 Itemised List of Possible Evidence on Alleged Contravention of the MARPOL Annex I Discharge Provisions

4.3.1 Action on Sighting Oil Pollution

1. Particulars of the vessel or vessels suspected of contravention
   - Name of the vessel
   - Reasons for suspecting the vessel
   - Date and time (UTC) of the observation or identification
   - Position of the vessel
   - Flag and port of registry
   - Type (for example, tanker, cargo vessel, passenger vessel, fishing vessel), size (estimated tonnage) and other descriptive data (for example, superstructure colour and funnel mark)
   - Draught condition (loaded or in ballast)
   - Approximate course and speed
   - Position of slick in relation to the vessel (for example, astern, port, starboard)
   - Part of the vessel from which side discharge was seen emanating
   - Whether the discharge ceased when the vessel was observed or contacted by radio.
2. Particulars of the slick
   - Date and time (UTC) of the observation if different from above
   - Position of the oil slick in longitude and latitude if different from above
   - Approximate distance in nautical miles from the nearest land

- Approximate overall dimension of the oil slick (i.e., length, width and percentage thereof covered by oil)
- Physical description of oil slick (i.e., direction and form, for example, continuous, in patches or in windrows)
- Appearance of the oil slick (indicate categories)
    - i. Category A: Barely visible under most favourable light condition
    - ii. Category B: Visible as silvery sheen on water surface
    - iii. Category C: First trace of colour may be observed
    - iv. Category D: Bright band of colour
    - v. Category E: Colours begin to turn dull
    - vi. Category F: Colours are much darker
- Sky conditions (bright sunshine, overcast, etc.), light fall and visibility (kilometres) at the time of observation
- Sea state
- Direction and speed of surface wind
- Direction and speed of current

3. Identification of the observer(s)

- Name of observer
- Organisation with which observer is affiliated (if any)
- Observer's status within the organisation
- Observation made from aircraft/vessel/shore/otherwise
- Name or identity of the vessel or aircraft from which observation was made
- Specific location of the vessel, aircraft, place on shore or otherwise from which observation was made
- Activity engaged in by observer when observation was made, for example, patrol, voyage, flight (en route from … to …)

4. Method of observation and documentation

- Visual
- Conventional photographs
- Remote sensing records and or remote sensing photographs
- Samples taken from slick
- Any other form of observation (specify)

Note: A photograph of the discharge should preferably be in colour. Photographs can provide the following information: that a material on the sea surface is oil; that the quantity of oil discharged does constitute a violation of the Convention; that the oil is being, or has been, discharged from a particular vessel; and the identity of the vessel. Experience has shown that can be obtained with the following three photographs:

- Details of the slick taken almost vertically down from an altitude of less than 300 m (984 feet) with the sun behind the photographer
- An overall view of the vessel and slick showing oil emanating from a particular vessel; and
- Details of the vessel for the purposes of identification.

5. Other information if radio contact can be established

- Vessel's master informed of pollution
- Explanation of the vessel's master
- Vessel's last port of call
- Vessel's next port of call
- Name of the vessel's master and owner
- Vessel's call sign.

4.3.2 Investigation on Board

1. Inspection of the IOPP Certificate
   - Name of the vessel
   - Distinctive number or letters
   - Port of registry
   - Type of vessel
   - Date and place of issue
   - Date and place of endorsement

   Note: If the vessel is not issued an IOPP Certificate, as much as possible of the requested information should be given.

2. Inspection of Supplement of the IOPP Certificate
   - Applicable paras of sections 2, 3, 4, 5 and 6 of the Supplement (non-oil tankers)
   - Applicable paras of sections 2, 3, 4, 5, 6, 7, 8, 9 and 10 of the Supplement (oil tankers)

   Note: If the vessel does not have an IOPP Certificate, a description should be given of the equipment and arrangements on board, designed to prevent marine pollution.

3. Inspection of the oil record book
   - Copy or print out sufficient pages of the oil record book—part I to cover a period of 30 days prior to the reported incident

- Copy or print out sufficient pages of the oil record book—part II (if on board) to cover a full loading/unloading/ballasting and tank cleaning cycle of the vessel. Also copy the tank diagram

4. Inspection of logbook
   - Last port, date of departure, draught forward and aft
   - Current port, date of arrival, draught forward and aft
   - Vessel's position at or near the time the incident was reported
   - Spot check if positions mentioned in the logbook agree with positions noted in the oil record book
5. Inspection of other documentation on board
   - Other documentation relevant for evidence (if necessary, make copies) such as:
     – recent ullage sheets
     – records of monitoring and control equipment
6. Inspection of the vessel
   - Vessel's equipment in accordance with the Supplement of the IOPP Certificate
   - Samples taken. State location on board
   - Traces of oil in vicinity of overboard discharge outlets
   - Condition of engine room and contents of bilges
   - Condition of oily water separator, filtering equipment and alarm, stopping or monitoring arrangements
   - Contents of sludge and or holding tanks
   - Sources of considerable leakage on oil tankers.
     The following additional evidence may be pertinent:
   - Oil on surface of segregated or dedicated clean ballast
   - Condition of pump-room bilges
   - Condition of COW system
   - Condition of inert gas (IG) system
   - Condition of monitoring and control system
   - Slop tank contents (estimate quantity of water and of oil)
7. Statements of persons concerned

   If the Oil Record Book—Part I has not been properly completed, information on the following questions may be pertinent:
   - Was there a discharge (accidental or intentional) at the time indicated on the incident report?
   - Is the bilge discharge controlled automatically?
   - If so, at what time was this system last put into operation and at what time was this system last put on manual mode?
   - If not, what were the date and time of the last bilge discharge?
   - What was the date of the last disposal of residue and how was disposal effected?
   - Is it usual to effect discharge of bilge water directly to the sea, or to store bilge water first in a collecting tank? Identify the collecting tank.

- Have oil fuel tanks recently been used as ballast tanks?

If the Oil Record Book—Part II has not been properly completed, information on the following questions may be pertinent:

- What was the cargo/ballast distribution in the vessel on departure from the last port?
- What was the cargo/ballast distribution in the vessel on arrival in the current port?
- When and where was the last loading effected?
- When and where was the last unloading effected?
- When and where was the last discharge of dirty ballast?
- When and where was the last cleaning of cargo tanks?
- When and where was the last crude oil washing operation and which tanks were washed?
- When and where was the last decanting of slop tanks?
- What is the ullage in the slop tanks and the corresponding height of interface?
- Which tanks contained the dirty ballast during the ballast voyage (if the vessel arrived in ballast)?
- Which tanks contained the clean ballast during the ballast voyage (if the vessel arrived in ballast)?

In addition, the following information may be pertinent:

- Details of the present voyage of the vessel (previous ports, next ports, trade)
- Contents of oil fuel and ballast tanks
- Previous and next bunkering, and type of oil fuel
- Availability or non-availability of reception facilities for oily wastes during the present voyage
- Internal transfer of oil fuel during the present voyage.

In the case of oil tankers, the following additional information may be pertinent:

- The trade the vessel is engaged in, such as short/long distance, crude or product or alternating crude/product, lightering service, oil/dry bulk
- Which tanks are clean and dirty
- Repairs carried out or envisaged in cargo tanks.

Miscellaneous information:

- Comments in respect of condition of the vessel's equipment
- Comments in respect of the pollution report
- Other comments.

4.3.3 Investigation Ashore

1. Analyses of oil samples
   Indicate method and results of the samples' analyses.
2. Further information
   Additional information on the vessel, obtained from oil terminal staff, tank cleaning contractors or shore reception facilities may be pertinent.

Note: Any information under this heading is, if practicable, to be corroborated by documentation such as signed statements, invoices, receipts.
3. Information not covered by the foregoing
4. Conclusion
   - Summing up of the investigator's technical conclusions
   - Indication of applicable provisions of MARPOL Annex I which the vessel is suspected of having contravened
   - Did the results of the investigation warrant the filing of a deficiency report?

4.4 In-Port Inspection of Crude Oil Washing Procedures

Guidelines for the in-port inspection of crude oil washing (COW) procedures, as called for by resolution 7 of the International Conference on Tanker Safety and Pollution Prevention, 1978, are required to provide a uniform and effective control of crude oil washing to always ensure compliance of vessels with the provisions of MARPOL. The design of the COW system installation is subject to the approval of the Flag Administration. However, although the operational aspect of crude oil washing is also subject to the approval of the same Administration, it might be necessary for a Port State Authority to see to it that continuing compliance with agreed procedures and parameters is ensured. The *COW Operations and Equipment Manual* has been so specified that it contains all the necessary information relating to the operation of crude oil washing on a particular tanker. The objectives of the inspection would then be to ensure that the provisions of the Manual dealing with safety procedures and with pollution prevention are being strictly adhered to. The method of the inspection is at the discretion of the Port State Authority and may cover the entire operation or only those parts of the operation which occur when the Port State Control Officer is on board. Port State Control Officer inspections are governed by Articles 5 and 6 of MARPOL.

4.4.1 Inspection Requirements

4.4.1.1 Inspections

Port States should make the appropriate arrangements so to ensure compliance with requirements governing the crude oil washing of oil tankers. This is not, however, to be construed as relieving terminal operators and shipowners of their obligations to ensure that the operation is undertaken in accordance with the regulations. The inspection may cover the entire operation of crude oil washing or only certain aspects of it. It is thus in the interest of all concerned that the vessel's records with respect to crude oil washing operations are accurately maintained so that a Port State Control Officer may verify those operations undertaken prior to the inspection.

4.4.1.2 Vessel's Personnel

The person in charge and the other nominated persons who have responsibility in respect of the crude oil washing operation should be identified. They must, if required, be able to show that their qualifications meet the requirements, as appropriate, of paras 5.2 and 5.3 of the *Revised specifications for the design, operation and control of crude oil washing systems* (resolution A.446(XI)), as amended. The verification may be accomplished by reference to the individual's discharge papers, testimonials issued by the vessel's operator or by certificates issued by a training centre approved by an Administration. The numbers of such personnel should be at least as stated in the Manual.

4.4.1.3 Documentation

The following documents should be made available for inspection:

1. IOPP Certificate and the Record of Construction and Equipment, to determine:
   - Whether the vessel is fitted with a crude oil washing system as required in regulation 33 of MARPOL Annex I
   - whether the COW system is in accordance to, and complying with, the requirements of regulations 33 and 35 of MARPOL Annex I
   - the validity and date of the Operations and Equipment Manual; and
   - the validity of the Certificate.
2. Approved Manual
3. Oil Record Book; and
4. Cargo Ship Safety Equipment Certificate to confirm that the inert gas system conforms to regulations contained in chapter II-2 of SOLAS 1974.

4.4.1.4 Inert Gas System

Inert gas system regulations require that instrumentation shall be fitted for continuously indicating and permanently always recording when inert gas is being supplied, the pressure and the oxygen content of the gas in the inert gas supply main. Reference to the permanent recorder would indicate if the system had been operating before and during the cargo discharge in a satisfactory manner. If conditions specified in the Manual are not being met, then the washing must be stopped until satisfactory conditions are restored. As a further precautionary measure, the oxygen level in each tank to be washed is to be determined at the tank. The meters used should be calibrated and inspected to ensure that they are in good working order. Readings from tanks already washed in port prior to inspection should be available for checking. Spot checks on readings may be instituted.

4.4.1.5 Electrostatic Generation

It should be confirmed either from the cargo log or by questioning the person in charge that the presence of water in the crude oil is being minimised as required by para 6.7 of

4.4 In-Port Inspection of Crude Oil Washing Procedures

the revised *Specifications for the design, operation and control of crude oil washing systems* (resolution A.446(XI)), as amended.

4.4.1.6 Communication
It should be established that effective means of communication exist between the person in charge and the other persons concerned with the crude oil washing operation.

4.4.1.7 Leakage on Deck
Port State Control Officers should ensure that the crude oil washing piping system has been operationally tested for leakage before cargo discharge and that the test has been noted in the vessel's Oil Record Book.

4.4.1.8 Exclusion of Oil from Engine Room
It should be ascertained that the method of excluding cargo oil from the machinery space is being maintained by inspecting the isolating arrangements of the tank washing heater (if fitted) or of any part of the tank washing system which enters the machinery space.

4.4.1.9 Suitability of the Crude Oil
In judging the suitability of the oil for crude oil washing, the guidance and criteria contained in section 9 of the *COW Operations and Equipment Manual* should be considered.

4.4.1.10 Checklist
It should be determined from the vessel's records that the pre-crude oil wash operational checklist was carried out and all instruments functioned correctly. Spot checks on certain items may be instituted.

4.4.2 Wash Programmes

Where the tanker is engaged in a multiple port discharge, the Oil Record Book would indicate if tanks were crude oil washed at previous discharge ports or at sea. It should be determined that all tanks which will or may be used to contain ballast on the forthcoming voyage will be crude oil washed before the vessel departs from the port. There is no obligation to wash any tank other than ballast tanks at a discharge port except that each of these other tanks must be washed at least in accordance with para 6.1 of the revised *Specifications for the design, operation and control of crude oil washing systems* (resolution A.446(XI)), as amended. The Oil Record Book should be inspected to check that this is being complied with. All crude oil washing must be completed before a vessel leaves its final port of discharge. If tanks are not being washed in one of the preferred orders given in the Manual, the Port State Control Officer should determine that the reason for this and the proposed order of tank washing are acceptable. For each tank being washed it should be ensured that the operation is in accordance with the Manual in that:

1. The deck-mounted machines and the submerged machines are operating either by reference to indicators, the sound patterns or other approved methods
2. The deck-mounted machines, where applicable, are programmed as stated
3. The duration of the wash is as required; and
4. The number of tank washing machines being used simultaneously does not exceed that specified.

4.4.3 Stripping of Tanks

The minimum trim conditions and the parameters of the stripping operations are to be stated in the Manual. All tanks which have been crude oil washed are to be stripped. The adequacy of the stripping is to be checked by hand dipping at least in the aftermost hand dipping location in each tank or by such other means provided and described in the Manual. It should be ascertained that the adequacy of stripping has been checked or will be checked before the vessel leaves its final port of discharge.

4.4.4 Ballasting

Tanks that were crude oil washed at sea will be recorded in the Oil Record Book. These tanks must be left empty between discharge ports for inspection at the next discharge port. Where these tanks are the designated departure ballast tanks they may be required to be ballasted at a very early stage of the discharge. This is for operational reasons and because they must be ballasted during cargo discharge if hydrocarbon emission is to be contained on the vessel. If these tanks are to be inspected when empty, then this must be done shortly after the tanker berths. If a Port State Control Officer arrives after the tanks have begun accepting ballast, then the sounding of the tank bottom would not be available. However, an examination of the surface of the ballast water is then possible. The thickness of the oil film should not be greater than that specified in para 4.2.10(b) of the revised *Specifications for the design, operation and control of crude oil washing systems* (resolution A.446(XI)), as amended. The tanks that are designated ballast tanks will be listed in the Manual. It is, however, left to the discretion of the vessel's master or responsible officer to decide which tanks may be used for ballast on the forthcoming voyage. It should be determined from the Oil Record Book that all such tanks have been washed before the tanker leaves its last discharge port. It should be noted that where a tanker back-loads a cargo of crude oil at an intermediate port into tanks designated for ballast, then it should not be required to wash those tanks at that port but at a subsequent

4.4 In-Port Inspection of Crude Oil Washing Procedures

port. It should be determined from the Oil Record Book that additional ballast water has not been put into tanks which have not been crude oil washed during previous voyages. It should be verified that the departure ballast tanks are stripped as completely as possible. Where departure ballast is filled through cargo lines and pumps these must be stripped either into another cargo tank or ashore by the special small diameter line provided for this purpose. The methods to avoid vapour emission where locally required will be provided in the Manual and they must be adhered to. The Port State Control Officer should ensure that this is being complied with. The typical procedures for ballasting listed in the Manual must be observed. The Port State Control Officer should ensure this is being complied with. When departure ballast is to be shifted, the discharge into the sea must comply with regulations 15 and 34 of MARPOL Annex I. The Oil Record Book should be inspected to ensure that the vessel is complying with this.

Investigations and Inspections Carried Out Under MARPOL Annex II

5.1 Inspection of Certificate (COF or NLS Certificate), Vessel and Equipment

5.1.1 Vessels Required to Hold a Certificate

On boarding and after introducing themselves to the vessel's master or the responsible vessel's officer, the Port State Control Officer should examine the Certificate of Fitness (COF) or NLS Certificate and Cargo Record Book (CRB). The Cargo Record Book may be presented in an electronic format. A declaration from the Administration should be viewed to accept this electronic record book. If a declaration cannot be provided, a hard copy record book will need to be presented for examination. The Certificate includes information on the type of vessel, the dates of surveys and a list of the products which the vessel is certified to carry. As a preliminary check, the Certificate's validity should be confirmed by verifying that the Certificate is properly completed and signed and that required surveys have been performed. In reviewing the Certificate, particular attention should be given to verifying that only those noxious liquid substances which are listed on the Certificate are carried and that these substances are in tanks approved for their carriage. The Cargo Record Book should be inspected to ensure that the records are up to date. The Port State Control Officer should check whether the vessel left the previous port(s) with residues of noxious liquid substances on board which could not be discharged into the sea. The book could also have relevant entries from the appropriate authorities in the previous ports. If the examination reveals that the vessel was permitted to sail from its last unloading port under certain conditions, the Port State Control Officer should ascertain that such conditions have been or will be adhered to. If the Port State Control Officer discovers an operational violation in this respect, the Flag State should be informed by means of a deficiency report. If the Certificate is valid and the Port State Control Officer's general impressions and visual observations on board confirm a good standard of maintenance, the Port State Control Officer should, provided that the Cargo Record Book entries do not show any operational violations, confine the inspection to reported deficiencies, if any. If, however, the Port State Control Officer's general impressions or observations on board show clear grounds for believing that the condition of the vessel, its equipment, or its cargo and slops handling operations do not correspond substantially with the particulars of the Certificate, the Port State Control Officer should proceed to a more detailed inspection:

1. Initially this requires an examination of the vessel's approved P and A Manual
2. The more detailed inspection should include the cargo and pump room areas of the vessel and should begin with forming a general impression of the layout of the tanks, the cargoes carried, pumping and stripping conditions and cargo
3. Next, a closer examination of the vessel's equipment as shown in the P and A Manual may take place. This examination should also confirm that no unapproved modifications have been made to the vessel and its equipment
4. Should any doubt arise as to the maintenance or the condition of the vessel or its equipment, further examination and testing may be conducted as may be necessary. In this respect reference is made to the *Survey Guidelines under the Harmonised System of Survey and Certification*, 2021 (resolution A.1156(32)), as may be amended.

The Port State Control Officer should bear in mind that a vessel may be equipped over and above the requirements of MARPOL Annex II. If such equipment is malfunctioning the Flag State should be informed. This alone, however, should not cause a vessel to be detained unless the malfunction presents an unreasonable threat of harm to the marine environment.

5.1.2 Vessels of Non-parties to the Convention

As this category of vessel is not provided with a COF or NLS Certificate as required by MARPOL Annex II, the Port State Control Officer should be satisfied with respect to the construction and equipment standards relevant to the vessel based on the requirements set out in MARPOL Annex II and the Standards for Procedures and Arrangements. In all other respects, the Port State Control Officer should be guided by the procedures for vessels referred to above (i.e., vessels required to hold a Certificate). If the vessel has some form of certification other than the required Certificate, the Port State Control Officer may take the form and content of this document into account in the evaluation of that vessel. Such a form of certification, however, is only of value to the Port State Control Officer if the vessel has been provided with a P and A Manual.

5.1.3 Control

In exercising the control functions, the Port State Control Officer should use professional judgement to determine whether to detain the vessel until any noted deficiencies are rectified or to allow it to sail with certain deficiencies which do not pose an unreasonable threat of harm to the marine environment. In doing this, the Port State Control Officer should be guided by the principle that the requirements contained in MARPOL Annex II, in respect of construction and equipment and the operation of vessels, are essential for the protection of the marine environment and that departure from these requirements could constitute an unreasonable threat of harm to the marine environment.

5.2 Contravention of Discharge Provisions

With illegal discharges, experience has shown that information furnished to the Flag State is often inadequate to enable the Flag State to cause proceedings to be brought in respect of the alleged violation of the discharge requirements. This chapter is intended to identify information which will be needed by a Flag State for the prosecution of violations of the discharge provisions under MARPOL Annex II. It is recommended that in preparing a Port State report on deficiencies, where contravention of the discharge requirements is involved, the authorities of a Coastal or Port State should be guided by the itemised list of possible evidence as shown later in this chapter. It should be borne in mind in this connection that:

1. The report aims to provide the optimal collation of obtainable data; however, even if all the information cannot be provided, as much information as possible should be submitted
2. It is important for all the information included in the report to be supported by facts which, when considered as a whole, would lead the Port or Coastal State to believe a contravention has occurred; and
3. The discharge may have been oil.

In addition to the Port State report on deficiencies, a report should be completed by a Port or Coastal State, based on the itemised list of possible evidence. It is important that these reports are supplemented by documents such as:

1. A statement by the observer of the pollution; in addition to the information required as stated in this chapter, the statement should include considerations which have led the observer to conclude that none of any other possible pollution sources is in fact the source

2. Statements concerning the sampling procedures both the slick and on board; these include location where and time when samples were taken, identity of person(s) taking the samples and receipts identifying the persons having custody and receiving transfer of the samples
3. Reports of analyses of samples taken of the slick and on board; the reports should include the results of the analyses, a description of the method employed, reference to or copies of scientific documentation attesting to the accuracy and validity of the method employed and names of persons performing the analyses and their experience
4. A statement by the Port State Control Officer on board together with their rank and organisation
5. Statements by persons being questioned
6. Statements by witnesses
7. Photographs of the slick; and
8. Copies or printouts of relevant pages of the Cargo Record Book, logbooks, discharge recordings, etc.

All observations, photographs and documentation should be supported by a signed verification of their authenticity. All certifications, authentications or verifications shall be executed in accordance with the laws of the State which prepares them. All statements should be signed and dated by the person making the statement and, if possible, by a witness to the signing. The names of the persons signing statements should be printed in legible script above or below the signature. The incident report should be sent to the Flag State. If the Coastal State observing the pollution and the Port State carrying out the investigation on board are not the same, the State carrying out the latter investigation should also send a copy of its findings to the State observing the pollution and requesting the investigation.

5.3 Itemised List of Possible Evidence on Alleged Contravention of the MARPOL Annex II Discharge Provisions

5.3.1 Action on Sighting Pollution

1. Particulars of the vessel or vessels suspected of contravention
   - Name of the vessel and IMO number
   - Reasons for suspecting the vessel
   - Date and time (UTC) of the observation or identification
   - Position of the vessel
   - Flag and port of registry

- Type, size (estimated tonnage) and other descriptive data (for example, superstructure colour and funnel mark)
- Draught condition (loaded or in ballast)
- Approximate course and speed
- Position of the slick in relation to vessel (for example, astern, port, starboard)
- Part of the vessel from which discharge was seen emanating
- Whether the discharge ceased when the vessel was observed or contacted by radio.

2. Particulars of the slick
   - Date and time (UTC) of the observation if different from above
   - Position of the slick in longitude and latitude if different from above
   - Approximate distance in nautical miles from the nearest land
   - Depth of water according to the sea chart
   - Approximate overall dimension of the slick (i.e., length, width and percentage thereof covered)
   - Physical description of the slick (direction and form, for example, continuous, in patches or in windrows)
   - Colour of the slick
   - Sky conditions (bright sunshine, overcast, etc.), light fall and visibility (kilometres) at the time of observation
   - Sea state
   - Direction and speed of surface wind
   - Direction and speed of current.

3. Identification of the observer(s)
   - Name of the observer
   - Organisation with which the observer is affiliated (if any)
   - Observer's status within the organisation
   - Observation made from a vessel, aircraft, shore or otherwise
   - Name or identity of the vessel or aircraft from which observation was made
   - Specific location of vessel, aircraft, place on shore or otherwise from which observation was made
   - Activity engaged in by the observer when observation was made, for example, patrol, voyage, flight (enroute from … to …).

4. Method of observation and documentation
   - Visual
   - Conventional photographs
   - Remote sensing records and or remote sensing photographs
   - Samples taken from the slick
   - Any other form of observation (specify).

   Note: A photograph of the discharge should preferably be in colour. The best results may be obtained with the following three photographs:

- details of the slick taken almost vertically down from an altitude of less than 300 m (984 feet) with the sun behind the photographer
  - an overall view of the vessel and slick showing a substance emanating from the particular vessel; and
  - details of the vessel for the purposes of identification.
5. Other information if radio contact can be established
   - Vessel master informed of the pollution
   - Explanation of the vessel's master
   - Vessel's last port of call
   - Vessel's next port of call
   - Name of the vessel's master and owner
   - Vessel's call sign.

5.3.2 Investigation on Board

1. Inspection of the Certificate (COF or NLS Certificate)
   - Name of the vessel and IMO number
   - Distinctive number or letters
   - Port of registry
   - Type of vessel
   - Date and place of issue
   - Date and place of endorsement
   - List of Annex II substances the vessel is certified to carry
   - Limitation as to tanks in which these substances may be carried.
2. Inspection of P and A Manual
   - Vessel equipped with an efficient stripping system
   - Residue quantities established at survey.
3. Inspection of Cargo Record Book

   Copy or print out sufficient pages of the Cargo Record Book to cover a full loading/unloading/ballasting and tank cleaning cycle of the vessel. It is also worth taking a copy of the tank diagram.
4. Inspection of logbook
   - Last port, date of departure, draught forward and aft
   - Current port, date of arrival, draught forward and aft
   - Vessel's position at or near the time the incident was reported
   - Spot check if times entered in the Cargo Record Book in respect of discharges correspond with sufficient distance from the nearest land, the required vessel's speed and with sufficient water depth.
5. Inspection of other documentation on board

   Other documentation relevant for evidence (if necessary, make copies) such as:

- cargo documents of cargo presently or recently carried, together with relevant information on required unloading temperature, viscosity and or melting point
- records of temperature of substances during unloading; and
- records of monitoring equipment if fitted.

6. Inspection of vessel
   - Vessel's equipment in accordance with the P and A Manual
   - Samples taken; state location on board
   - Sources of considerable leakage
   - Cargo residues on surface of segregated or dedicated clean ballast
   - Condition of pump room bilges
   - Condition of monitoring system
   - Slop tank contents (estimate quantity of water and residues).
7. Statements of persons concerned (if the Cargo Record Book has not been properly completed, information on the following questions may be pertinent)
   - Was there a discharge (accidental or intentional) at the time indicated on the incident report?
   - Which tanks are going to be loaded in the port?
   - Which tanks needed cleaning at sea? Had the tanks been prewashed?
   - When and where were these cleaned?
   - Residues of which substances were involved?
   - What was done with the tank washing slops?
   - Was the slop tank, or cargo tank used as a slop tank, discharged at sea?
   - When and where was the discharge effected?
   - What are the contents of the slop tank or cargo tank used as slop tank?
   - Which tanks contained the dirty ballast during the ballast voyage (i.e., if the vessel arrived in ballast)?
   - Which tanks contained the clean ballast during the ballast voyage (i.e., if the vessel arrived in ballast)?
   - Details of the present voyage of the vessel (previous ports, next ports, trade)
   - Difficulties experienced with discharge to shore reception facilities
   - Difficulties experienced with efficient stripping operations
   - Which tanks are clean or dirty on arrival?
   - Repairs carried out or envisaged in cargo tanks
   - Miscellaneous information
   - Comments in respect of condition of vessel's equipment
   - Comments in respect of pollution report
   - Other comments.

5.3.3 Investigation Ashore

1. Analyses of samples

Indicate method and results of the samples' analyses.
2. Further information

   Additional information on the vessel, obtained from terminal staff, tank cleaning contractors or shore reception facilities, may be pertinent.

   Note: Any information under this heading is, if practicable, to be corroborated by documentation such as signed statements, invoices, receipts.
3. Information from previous unloading port terminal
   - Confirmation that the vessel was unloaded, stripped or prewashed in accordance with its P and A Manual
   - The nature of difficulties (if any)
   - Restrictions by authorities under which the vessel was permitted to sail
   - Restrictions in respect of shore reception facilities.
4. Information not covered by the foregoing.

5.4 Conclusion

- Summing up of the investigator's conclusions
- Indication of applicable provisions of MARPOL Annex II which the vessel is suspected of having contravened
- Did the results of the investigation warrant the filing of a deficiency report?

5.5 Procedures for Inspection of Unloading, Stripping and Prewashing Operations (Mainly in Unloading Ports)

The Port State Control Officer or the surveyor authorised by the Administration exercising control in accordance with regulation 16 of MARPOL Annex II should be thoroughly acquainted with MARPOL Annex II and the custom of the port as of relevance to cargo handling, tank washing, cleaning berths, prohibition of lighters alongside, etc.

5.5.1 Documentation

The documentation required for the inspection referred to in this appendix consists of:

1. COF or NLS Certificate
2. Cargo plan and shipping document
3. P and A Manual; and the
4. Cargo Record Book.

5.5.2 Information by Vessel's Staff

Of relevance to the Port State Control Officer or the surveyor appointed or authorised by the Administration is the following:

1. The intended loading and unloading programme of the vessel
2. Whether unloading and stripping operations can be carried out in accordance with the P and A Manual and if not the reason why it cannot be done
3. The constraints, if any, under which the efficient stripping system operates (i.e., back pressure, ambient air temperature, malfunctioning, etc.); and
4. Whether the vessel requests an exemption from the prewashing and the discharge of residues in the unloading port.

When tank washing is required without the use of water the Port State Control Officer, or the surveyor appointed or authorised by the Administration is to be informed about the tank washing procedure and disposal of residues. When the Cargo Record Book is not up to date, any information on prewash and residue disposal operations outstanding should be supplied.

5.5.3 Information from Terminal Staff

Terminal staff should supply information on limitations imposed upon the vessel in respect of back pressure and or reception facilities.

5.5.4 Control

On boarding and introduction to the vessel's master or responsible vessel officers, the Port State Control Officer or the surveyor appointed or authorised by the Administration should examine the necessary documentation. The documentation may be used to establish the following:

1. Noxious liquid substances to be unloaded, their categories and stowage (cargo plan, P and A Manual)
2. Details of efficient stripping system, if fitted (P and A Manual)
3. Tanks which require prewashing with disposal of tank washings to reception facilities (shipping document and cargo temperature)
4. Tanks which require prewashing with disposal of tank washings either to reception facilities or into the sea (P and A Manual, shipping document and cargo temperature)

5. Prewash operations and or residue disposal operations outstanding (Cargo Record Book); and
6. Tanks which may not be washed with water due to the nature of substances involved (P and A Manual).

In respect of the prewash operations referred above, the following information is of relevance (P and A Manual):

1. Pressure required for tank washing machines
2. Duration of one cycle of the tank washing machine and quantity of water used
3. Washing programmes for the substances involved
4. Required temperature of washing water; and
5. Special procedures.

The Port State Control Officer or the surveyor authorised by the Administration, in accordance with regulation 16 of MARPOL Annex II, should ascertain that unloading, stripping and or prewash operations are carried out in conformity with the information. If this cannot be achieved, alternative measures should be taken to ensure that the vessel does not proceed to sea with more than the quantities of residue specified in regulation 12 of MARPOL Annex II, as applicable. If the residue quantities cannot be reduced by alternative measures the Port State Control Officer or the surveyor appointed or authorised by the Administration should inform the Port State Administration. Care should be taken to ensure that cargo hoses and piping systems of the terminal are not drained back to the vessel. If a vessel is exempted from certain pumping efficiency requirements under regulation 4.4 of MARPOL Annex II or requests an exemption from certain stripping or prewashing procedures under regulation 13.4 of MARPOL Annex II, the conditions for such exemption set out in the said regulations should be observed. These relate to:

1. *Regulations 4.2 and 4.3*: the vessel is constructed before 1 July 1986 and is exempted from the requirement for reducing its residue quantities to specified limits of regulation 12 (i.e. category X or Y substances 300 L and category Z substances 900 L); this is subject to the conditions of regulation 4.3 that whenever a cargo tank is to be washed or ballasted, a prewash is required with disposal of prewash slops to shore reception facilities; the COF or NLS Certificate should have been endorsed to the effect that the vessel is solely engaged in restricted voyages
2. *Regulation 4.4*: the vessel is never required to ballast its cargo tanks and tank washing is only required for repair or drydocking; the COF or NLS Certificate should indicate the particulars of the exemption; each cargo tank should be certified for the carriage of only one named substance
3. *Regulation 13.4.1*: cargo tanks will not be washed or ballasted prior to the next loading

4. *Regulation 13.4.2*: cargo tanks will be washed, and prewash slops will be discharged to reception facilities in another port; it should be confirmed in writing that an adequate reception facility is available at that port for such purpose; and
5. *Regulation 13.4.3*: the cargo residues can be removed by ventilation.

The Port State Control Officer or the surveyor appointed or authorised by the Administration must endorse the Cargo Record Book under section J whenever an exemption under regulation 13.4 has been granted, or whenever a tank having unloaded category X substances has been prewashed in accordance with the P and A Manual. Alternatively, for category X substances, regulation 13.6.1.1 of MARPOL Annex II, residual concentration should be measured by the procedures which each Port State authorises. In this case the Port State Control Officer or the surveyor authorised by the Administration must endorse in the Cargo Record Book under section K whenever the required residual concentration has been achieved. In addition, the Port State Control Officer or the surveyor authorised by the Administration will endorse the Cargo Record Book whenever the unloading, stripping or prewash of category Y and Z substances, in accordance with the P and A Manual, has been witnessed. With reference to endorsements 5.7, 8, 9 if the vessel has implemented an electronic record book, the shipowner may request these endorsements using a stand-alone form or request of a copy of the surveyor's report to accompany the electronic record book entry.

Discharge Requirements Under MARPOL Annexes I and II

Regulations 15 and 34 of MARPOL Annex I prohibit the discharge into the sea of oil and regulation 13 of Annex II prohibits the discharge into the sea of noxious liquid substances except under precisely defined conditions. A record of these operations shall be completed, where appropriate, in the form of an Oil or Cargo Record Book as applicable and shall be kept in such a place as to be readily available for inspection at all reasonable times. The regulations referred to above provide that whenever visible traces of oil are observed on or below the surface of the water in the immediate vicinity of a vessel or of its wake, a Party should, to the extent that it is reasonably able to do so, promptly investigate the facts bearing on the issue of whether there has been a violation of the discharge provisions. The conditions under which noxious liquid substances are permitted to be discharged into the seas include quantity, quality and position limitations, which depend on category of substance and sea area. An investigation into an alleged contravention should therefore aim to establish whether a noxious liquid substance has been discharged and whether the operations leading to that discharge were in accordance with the vessel's Procedures and Arrangements Manual (P and A Manual). Recognising the likelihood that many of the violations of the discharge provisions will take place outside the immediate control and knowledge of the Flag State, Article 6 of MARPOL provides that Parties should cooperate in the detection of violations and the enforcement of the provisions using all appropriate and practicable measures of detection and environmental monitoring, and adequate procedures for reporting and gathering evidence. MARPOL also contains several more specific provisions designed to facilitate that cooperation. Several sources of information about possible violations of the discharge provisions can be indicated. These include:

1. *Reports by vessel's masters*: Article 8 and Protocol I of MARPOL require, inter alia, a vessel's master to report certain incidents involving the discharge or the probability of a discharge of oil or oily mixtures, or noxious liquid substances or mixtures containing such substances
2. *Reports by official bodies*: Article 8 of MARPOL requires furthermore that a Party issues instructions to its maritime inspection vessels and aircraft and to other appropriate services to report to its authorities incidents involving the discharge or the probability of a discharge of oil or oily mixtures, or noxious liquid substances or mixtures containing such substances
3. *Reports by other Parties*: Article 6 of MARPOL provides that a Party may request another Party to inspect a vessel; the Party making the request shall supply sufficient evidence that the vessel has discharged oil or oily mixtures, noxious liquid substances or mixtures containing such substances, or that the vessel has departed from the unloading port with residues of noxious liquid substances in excess of those permitted to be discharged into the sea; and
4. *Reports by others*: it is not possible to list exhaustively all sources of information concerning alleged contravention of the discharge provisions; Parties should take all circumstances into account when deciding upon investigating such reports.

Action which can be taken by States other than the Flag or Port States that have information on discharge violations (hereinafter referred to as Coastal States):

1. Coastal States that are Parties to MARPOL, upon receiving a report of pollution by oil or noxious liquid substances allegedly caused by a vessel, may investigate the matter and collect such evidence as can be collected; for details of the desired evidence, refer to Chap. 4
2. If the investigation discloses that the next port of call of the vessel in question lies within its jurisdiction, the Coastal State should also take Port State action
3. If the investigation discloses that the next port of call of the vessel in question lies within the jurisdiction of another Party, then the Coastal State should in appropriate cases furnish the evidence to that other Party and request that Party to take Port State action; and
4. In either case referred to in points 2 and 3 above and if the next port of call of the vessel in question cannot be ascertained, the Coastal State should inform the Flag State of the incident and of the evidence obtained.

6.1 Port State Action

Parties should appoint or authorise officers to carry out investigations for the purpose of verifying whether a vessel has discharged oil or noxious liquid substances in violation of the provisions of MARPOL. Parties may undertake such investigations based on reports received from sources indicated in points 1 to 4 above. These investigations should be directed towards the gathering of sufficient evidence to establish whether the vessel has violated the discharge requirements. Guidelines for the optimal collation of evidence are provided later. If the investigations provide evidence that a violation of the discharge requirements took place within the jurisdiction of the Port State, that Port State shall either cause proceedings to be taken in accordance with its law or furnish to the Flag State all information and evidence in its possession about the alleged violation. When the Port State causes proceedings to be taken, it shall inform the Flag State. Details of the report to be submitted to the Flag State are set out in appendix 16. The investigation might provide evidence that pollution was caused through damage to the vessel or its equipment. This might indicate that a vessel is not guilty of a violation of the discharge requirements of MARPOL Annex I or Annex II provided that:

- All reasonable precautions have been taken after the occurrence of the damage or discovery of the discharge for the purpose of preventing or minimising the discharge; and
- The owner or the vessel's master did not act either with intent to cause damage or recklessly and with knowledge that damage would probably result.

However, action by the Port State as set out in Chap. 3 may still be warranted if the circumstances allow.

6.2 Inspection of Crude Oil Washing Operations

Regulations 18, 33 and 35 of MARPOL Annex I inter alia require that crude oil washing of cargo tanks be performed on certain categories of crude carriers. A sufficient number of tanks shall be washed in order that ballast water is put only in cargo tanks which have been crude oil washed. The remaining cargo tanks shall be washed on a rotational basis for sludge control. Port State Authorities may carry out inspections to ensure that crude oil washing is performed by all crude carriers either required to have a COW system or where the owner or operator chooses to install a COW system to comply with regulation 18 of MARPOL Annex I. In addition, compliance should be ensured with the operational requirements set out in the *Revised specifications for the design, operation and control of crude oil washing systems* (resolution A.446(XI), as amended). This can best be done in the ports where the cargo is unloaded. Parties should be aware that the inspection may also lead to the identification of a pollution risk, necessitating additional action by the Port State as set out in Chap. 3 of this book. Detailed guidelines for in-port inspections of crude oil washing procedures have been approved and published by the IMO (Crude Oil Washing Systems, revised edition, 2000) and are summarised later in this chapter.

6.3 Inspection of Unloading, Stripping and Prewash Operations

Regulation 16 of MARPOL Annex II requires Parties to MARPOL to appoint or authorise surveyors for the purpose of implementing the regulation. The provisions of regulation 16 are aimed at ensuring in principle that a vessel having unloaded, to the maximum possible extent, noxious liquid substances of category X, Y or Z, proceeds to sea only if residues of such substances have been reduced to such quantities as may be discharged into the sea. Compliance with these provisions is in principle ensured in the case of categories X, Y and Z substances through the application of a prewash in the unloading port and the discharge of prewash residue water mixtures to reception facilities, except that, in the case of non-solidifying and low viscosity categories Y and Z substances, requirements for the efficient stripping of a tank to negligible quantities apply in lieu of the application of a prewash. Alternatively, for several substances ventilation procedures may be employed for removing cargo residues from a tank. Regulation 16.6 permits the Government of the receiving Party to exempt a vessel proceeding to a port or terminal under the jurisdiction of another Party from the requirement to prewash cargo tanks and discharge residue/water mixtures to a reception facility. Existing chemical tankers engaged on restricted voyages may by virtue of regulation 4.3 of MARPOL Annex II be exempted from the quantity limitation requirements of regulations 12.1 to 12.3. If a cargo tank is to be ballasted or washed, a prewash is required after unloading category Y or Z substances and prewash residue water mixtures must be discharged to shore reception facilities. The exemption should be indicated on the certificate.

A vessel whose constructional and operational features are such that ballasting of cargo tanks is not required and cargo tank washing is only required for repairs or dry-docking may by virtue of regulation 4.4 be exempted from the provisions of regulation 12 of MARPOL Annex II, provided that all conditions mentioned in regulation 4.4 are complied with. Accordingly, the certificate of the vessel should indicate that each cargo tank is only certified for the carriage of one named substance. It should also indicate the particulars of the exemption granted by the Administration in respect of pumping, piping and discharge arrangements. Detailed instructions on efficient stripping and prewash procedures are included in a vessel's P and A Manual. The Manual also contains alternative procedures to be followed in case of equipment failure. Parties should be aware that the

6.3 Inspection of Unloading, Stripping and Prewash Operations

inspection referred to in the section above may lead to the identification of a pollution risk or of a contravention of the discharge provisions, necessitating Port State action as set out in Chap. 3. For details in respect of inspections under this section, reference may be made to Chap. 5.

7 More Detailed Inspections for Vessel Structural and Equipment Requirements

If the Port State Control Officer from general impressions or observations on board has clear grounds for believing that the vessel might be substandard, the Port State Control Officer should proceed to a more detailed inspection, taking the following considerations into account:

- Conditions of the vessel's structure
- Conditions of machinery spaces
- Conditions of assignment of load lines
- Lifesaving appliances
- Fire safety
- Application of the regulations for preventing collisions at sea (COLREGs)
- Cargo vessel safety construction certificate
- Cargo vessel safety radio certificate
- Means of access to the vessel; and
- Any equipment in excess of convention or Flag State requirements.

7.1 Considerations for Detailed Inspections

7.1.1 Conditions of the Vessel's Structure

The Port State Control Officer's impression of hull maintenance and the general state on deck, the condition of such items as ladderways, guard rails, pipe coverings and areas of corrosion or pitting should influence the Port State Control Officer's decision as to whether it is necessary to make the fullest possible examination of the structure with the vessel afloat. Significant areas of damage or corrosion or pitting of plating and associated stiffening in decks and hull affecting seaworthiness or strength to take local loads, may justify detention. It may be necessary for the underwater portion of the vessel to be checked. In reaching a decision, the Port State Control Officer should have regard to the seaworthiness and not the age of the vessel, making an allowance for fair wear and tear over the minimum acceptable scantlings. Damage not affecting seaworthiness will not constitute grounds for judging that a vessel should be detained, nor will damage that has been temporarily but effectively repaired for a voyage to a port for permanent repairs. However, in this assessment of the effect of damage, the Port State Control Officer should have regard to the location of crew accommodation and whether the damage substantially affects its habitability. The Port State Control Officer should pay particular attention to the structural integrity and seaworthiness of bulk carriers and oil tankers and note that these vessels must undergo the enhanced programme of inspection during surveys under the provision of SOLAS 1974 regulation XI-1/2. The Port State Control Officer's assessment of the safety of the structure of those vessels should be based on the Survey Report File carried on board. This file should contain reports of structural surveys, condition evaluation reports (translated into English and endorsed by or on behalf of the Administration), thickness measurement reports and a survey planning document. The Port State Control Officer should note that there may be a short delay in the update of the Survey Report File following survey. Where there is doubt that the required survey has taken place, the Port State Control Officer should seek confirmation from the RO. If the Survey Report File necessitates a more detailed inspection of the structure of the vessel or if no such report is carried, special attention should be given by the Port State Control Officer, as appropriate, to hull structure, piping systems in way of cargo tanks or holds, pump rooms, cofferdams, pipe tunnels, void spaces within the cargo area and ballast tanks. For bulk carriers, Port State Control Officers should inspect holds' main structure for any obviously unauthorised repairs. For bulk carriers, the Port State Control Officer should verify that the bulk carrier booklet has been endorsed, the water level alarms in cargo holds are fitted, and where applicable, that any restrictions imposed on the carriage of solid bulk cargoes have been recorded in the booklet and the bulk carrier loading triangle is permanently marked.

7.1.2 Conditions of Machinery Spaces

The Port State Control Officer should assess the condition of the machinery and of the electrical installations such that they can provide sufficient continuous power for propulsion and for auxiliary services. During inspection of the machinery spaces, the Port State Control Officer should form an impression of the standard of maintenance. Frayed, disconnected or inoperative quick-closing valve wires, disconnected or inoperative extended control rods or machinery trip mechanisms, missing valve hand wheels, evidence of

7.1 Considerations for Detailed Inspections

chronic steam, water and oil leaks, dirty tank tops and bilges or extensive corrosion of machinery foundations are pointers to an unsatisfactory organisation of the systems' maintenance. A large number of temporary repairs, including pipe clips or cement boxes, will indicate reluctance to make permanent repairs. While it is not possible to determine the condition of the machinery without performance trials, general deficiencies, such as leaking pump glands, dirty water gauge glasses, inoperable pressure gauges, rusted relief valves, inoperative or disconnected safety or control devices, evidence of repeated operation of diesel engine scavenge belt or crankcase relief valves, malfunctioning or inoperative automatic equipment and alarm systems, and leaking boiler casings or uptakes, would warrant inspection of the engine room logbook and investigation into the record of machinery failures and accidents and a request for running tests of machinery. If one electrical generator is out of commission, the Port State Control Officer should investigate whether power is available to maintain essential and emergency services and should conduct tests. If evidence of neglect becomes evident, the Port State Control Officer should extend the scope of an investigation to include, for example, tests on the main and auxiliary steering gear arrangements, overspeed trips, circuit breakers. It must be stressed that while detection of one or more of the above deficiencies would afford guidance to a substandard condition, the actual combination is a matter for professional judgement in each case.

7.1.3 Conditions of Assignment of Load Lines

It may be that the Port State Control Officer has concluded that a hull inspection is unnecessary but, if dissatisfied on the basis of observations on deck, with items such as defective hatch closing arrangements, corroded air pipes and vent coamings, the Port State Control Officer should examine closely the conditions of assignment of load lines, paying particular attention to closing appliances, means of freeing water from the deck and arrangements concerned with the protection of the crew.

7.1.4 Lifesaving Appliances

The effectiveness of lifesaving appliances depends heavily on good maintenance by the crew and their use in regular drills. The lapse of time since the last survey for a Safety Equipment Certificate (SEC) can be a significant factor in the degree of deterioration of equipment if it has not been subject to regular inspection by the crew. Apart from failure to carry equipment required by a convention or obvious defects such as holed lifeboats, the Port State Control Officer should look for signs of disuse of, obstructions to, or defects with survival craft launching and recovery equipment, which may include paint accumulation, seizing of pivot points, absence of greasing, condition of blocks and falls, condition of lifeboat lifting hook attachment to the lifeboat hull and improper lashing or stowing of deck cargo. Should such signs be evident, the Port State Control Officer would be justified in making a detailed inspection of all lifesaving appliances. Such an examination might include the lowering of survival craft, a check on the servicing of life rafts, the number and condition of lifejackets and lifebuoys and ensuring that the pyrotechnics are still within their period of validity. It would not normally be as detailed as that for a renewal of the Safety Equipment Certificate and would concentrate on essentials for safe abandonment of the vessel, but in an extreme case could progress to a full Safety Equipment Certificate inspection. The provision and functioning of effective overside lighting, means of alerting the crew and passengers and provision of illuminated routes to assembly points and embarkation positions should be given importance in the inspection.

7.1.5 Fire Safety

Vessels in general: The poor condition of fire and wash deck lines and hydrants and the possible absence of fire hoses and extinguishers in accommodation spaces might be a guide to a need for a close inspection of all fire safety equipment. In addition to compliance with convention requirements, the Port State Control Officer should look for evidence of a higher fire risk than normal; this might be brought about by a poor standard of cleanliness in the machinery space, which together with significant deficiencies of fixed or portable fire extinguishing equipment could lead to a judgement of the vessel being substandard. Queries on the method of structural protection should be addressed to the Flag Administration and the Port State Control Officer should generally confine the inspection to the effectiveness of the arrangements provided.

Passenger vessels: The Port State Control Officer should initially form an opinion of the need for inspection of the fire safety arrangements based on consideration of the vessel under the previous headings and, in particular, that dealing with fire safety equipment. If the Port State Control Officer considers that a more detailed inspection of fire safety arrangements is necessary, the Port State Control Officer should examine the fire control plan on board to obtain a general picture of the fire safety measures provided in the vessel and consider their compliance with convention requirements for the year of build. Queries on the method of structural protection should be addressed to the Flag Administration and the Port State Control Officer should generally confine the inspection to the effectiveness of the arrangements provided. The spread of fire could be accelerated if fire doors are not readily operable. The Port State Control Officer should inspect for the operability and securing arrangements of those doors in the main zone bulkheads and stairway enclosures and in boundaries of high fire risk spaces, such as main machinery rooms and galleys, giving particular attention to those retained in the open position. Attention should also be given to main vertical zones which may have been compromised through new construction. An additional hazard in the event of fire is the spread of smoke through ventilation systems. Spot checks might be made on dampers and smoke flaps to ascertain the standard of operability. The Port State Control Officer should also ensure that ventilation fans can be stopped from the vessel's master controls and that means are available for closing main inlets and outlets of ventilation systems. Attention should be given to the effectiveness of escape routes by ensuring that vital doors are not kept locked, and that alleyways and stairways are not obstructed. Regarding the minimum width of external escape routes, the arrangements approved by the Flag Administrations should be accepted. The arrangements for the location of manually operated call points as approved by the Flag Administrations should be accepted.

7.1.6 Application of the Regulations for Preventing Collisions at Sea (COLREGs)

A vital aspect of ensuring safety of life at sea is full compliance with the collision regulations. Based on observations on deck, the Port State Control Officer should consider the need for close inspection of lanterns and their screening and means of making sound and distress signals.

7.1.7 Cargo Ship Safety Construction Certificate

The general condition of the vessel may lead the Port State Control Officer to consider matters other than those concerned with safety equipment and assignment of load lines, but nevertheless associated with the safety of the vessel, such as the effectiveness of items associated with the Cargo Ship Safety Construction Certificate, which can include pumping arrangements, means for shutting off air and oil supplies in the event of fire, alarm systems and emergency power supplies.

7.1.8 Cargo Ship Safety Radio Certificates

The validity of the Cargo Ship Safety Radio Certificates and associated Record of Equipment (Form R) may be accepted as proof of the provision and effectiveness of its associated equipment, but the Port State Control Officer should ensure that appropriate certificated personnel are carried for its operation and for listening periods. Requirements for maintenance of radio equipment are contained in SOLAS 1974 regulation IV/15. The radio log or radio records should be examined. Where considered necessary, operational checks may be carried out.

7.1.9 Means of Access to Vessel

Prior to boarding a vessel, the Port State Control Officer should assess the means of embarkation on and disembarkation from the vessel. The Port State Control Officer should be guided by SOLAS 1974 regulation II-1/3-9, noting its application to vessels constructed on or after 1 January 2010, but also noting that para 3 of this regulation applies to all vessels and requires that:

1. The means of embarkation and disembarkation shall be inspected and maintained in suitable condition for their intended purpose, taking account of any restrictions related to safe loading; and
2. All wires used to support the means of embarkation and disembarkation shall be maintained as specified in SOLAS 1974 regulation III/20.4.

In respect to the maintenance of the means of embarkation and disembarkation, the Port State Control Officer should refer to the *Guidelines for construction, installation, maintenance and inspection/survey of means of embarkation and disembarkation* (MSC.1/Circ.1331). During the inspection, the Port State Control Officer should also ensure that the pilot transfer arrangements comply with SOLAS 1974 regulation V/23 and the Unified interpretation of SOLAS regulation V/23 (MSC.1/Circ.1375/Rev.1 and MSC.1/Circ.1495/Rev.1).

7.1.10 Equipment in Excess of Convention or Flag State Requirements

Equipment on board which is expected to be relied on in situations affecting safety or pollution prevention must be in operating condition. If such equipment is inoperative and is in excess of the equipment required by an appropriate convention and or the Flag State, it should be repaired, removed or, if removal is not practicable, clearly marked as inoperative and secured.

Control of Operational Requirements

8.1 Inspection Processes

When, during a Port State Control inspection, the Port State Control Officer has clear grounds (refer to Chap. 1) the following onboard operational procedures may be checked in accordance with this resolution. However, in exercising Port State Control authority, the Port State Control Officer should not include any operational tests or impose physical demands which, in the judgement of the vessel's master, could jeopardise the safety of the vessel, crew, passengers, control officers or cargo. Prior to requiring any practical operational control, the Port State Control Officer should review training and drill records and should inspect, as appropriate, the associated safety equipment and its maintenance records. For example, an enclosed space entry drill may be sufficiently verified without an actual enclosed space entry by verifying drill records, maintenance records, physical inspection and physical demonstrations by crew of breathing apparatus, safety harnesses and atmosphere testing instruments. When carrying out operational control, the Port State Control Officer should ensure, as far as possible, no interference with normal shipboard operations, such as loading and unloading of cargo and ballasting, which is carried out under the responsibility of the vessel's master, nor should the Port State Control Officer require demonstration of operational aspects which would unnecessarily delay the vessel. Having assessed the extent to which operational requirements are complied with, the Port State Control Officer then should exercise their professional judgement to determine whether the operational proficiency of the crew is of a sufficient level to allow the vessel to sail without danger to the vessel or persons on board, or without presenting an unreasonable threat of harm to the marine environment. When assessing the crew's ability to conduct an operational drill, the mandatory minimum requirements for familiarisation and basic safety training for seafarers, as stated in STCW 1978, as amended, shall be used as a benchmark.

8.1.1 Definitions and Abbreviations

The definitions and abbreviations used in this chapter are those contained below:

- *Operational control*: A control inspection to confirm the vessel's master and crew are familiar with essential shipboard procedures with respect to the safety of the vessel and crew and protection of the environment and can apply such procedures. It includes a check on the effectiveness of communication and interaction and familiarity of the crew, including the human interface
- *Functional test*: A test of an item to prove the correct operation and function of equipment. Functional tests may be carried out during an initial or more detailed inspection.

8.2 More Detailed Inspection for Operational Requirements

A more detailed inspection should assess the ability of relevant crew to operate essential shipboard equipment that is relevant to their role. The responsible crew member must be able to operate such equipment independent of others and care must be taken to ensure they are not coached through the process when asked to demonstrate their understanding. A more detailed inspection should assess the familiarity of crew to essential shipboard procedures relevant to their role, the safety of the vessel and the protection of the environment. The Port State Control Officer should make an overall assessment of the effectiveness of communication and interaction and familiarity of the crew, including the human interface. The Port State Control Officer can use the items in Sect. 5 below as guidance in assessing the ability of the vessel's master or crew member to operate the vessel. The desired outcome is to effectively assess compliance with operational requirements in order that corrective action(s) may be applied where necessary.

8.2.1 Drills

A more detailed inspection may include drills. Where drills are to be conducted these should be carried out at a safe pace. Port State Control Officer should not expect to see operational activities including drills conducted in real time. Care should be taken to ensure that all crew familiarises themselves with their duties and with the equipment. If necessary, drills should be stopped or suspended if the Port State Control Officer considers that the crew are carrying out unsafe practices or if there is a real emergency. In addition, the following should be considered:

8.2 More Detailed Inspection for Operational Requirements 69

1. The Port State Control Officer should devise the emergency scenario on which a drill will be based in conjunction with the vessel's master. Experience has shown that the best assessment is achieved when the Port State Control Officer devises and controls the scenario, (in collaboration with the vessel's master) since there is then an element of uncertainty on the part of the vessel's officers as to how a drill will progress and is more realistic to the actual onboard situation facing crew members in a critical situation; and
2. It is essential that meetings are held between the Port State Control Officer and key members of the vessel's personnel before and after any operational activity involving multiple crew members. An initial briefing should be used to explain in general terms how the activity will be conducted and should also enable the vessel's staff to recognise the Port State Control Officer who are witnessing the activity, it is recommended that all Port State Control Officer witnessing the drill wear distinctive high visibility clothing to distinguish them from crew members.

8.2.2 Meeting on Inspection Outcomes and Findings with Respect to Operational Requirements

At the conclusion of the inspection a meeting should held with the vessel's master to ensure there is a common understanding of the outcomes and any findings of the detailed inspection, to identify any shortcomings and, if appropriate, where operational activity did not meet the required standard.

8.2.3 Communication

The Port State Control Officer may determine if the key crew members are able to communicate with each other, and with passengers, as appropriate, in such a way that the safe operation of the vessel is not impaired, especially in emergency situations. The Port State Control Officer may ask the vessel's master which languages are used as the working languages and may verify whether the language has been recorded in the logbook. The Port State Control Officer may ensure that the key crew members are able to understand each other during the inspection or drills. The crew members assigned to assist passengers should be able to give the necessary information to the passengers in case of an emergency. Language difficulty between the Port State Control Officer and non-English-speaking crews can make it difficult to put across the intentions for the conduct of the inspection and any associated drills. Care needs to be exercised when an unsatisfactory inspection outcome is found to ensure there is a differentiation between the miscommunication between the Port State Control Officer and the crew and failure of operational requirements. Passenger vessels constructed on or after 1 July 2010 shall have on board a safety centre. The safety centre shall either be a part of the navigation bridge or be in a separate space adjacent but having direct access to the navigation bridge. The Port State Control Officer should verify effective means of communication between the safety centre, the central control station, the navigation bridge, the engine control room, the storage room(s) for fire extinguishing system(s) and fire equipment lockers are provided.

8.2.4 Assessing the Vessel with Respect to Operational Requirements

If any of the following are found during a more detailed inspection a detention of the vessel may be considered:

1. Failure of deck officers and crew to monitor cargo loading operations and take precautions appropriate to that cargo
2. Lack of awareness of the operation of, and limitations of, navigation equipment or how to test such equipment (including navigation lights)
3. Deck officers unable to demonstrate the operation of essential navigation equipment such as ECDIS and integrated navigations systems. This includes the monitoring and interrogating alarms on such systems
4. There is evidence that the vessel's navigation has been carried out in an unsafe manner including, but not limited to:
   - Failure to monitor the vessels position in accordance with shipboard procedures
   - Failure to verify the accuracy of position fixing through use of multiple means of obtaining fixes
   - Failure to properly plan and assess a voyage
   - Navigating the vessel into danger or into restricted areas
   - Deck officers unfamiliar with the operation and testing of radio communications equipment and or the mechanism by which marine safety information is provided to the vessel
   - Relevant officers and crew unfamiliar with the locations of the starting positions or the starting operation of the firefighting equipment such as the emergency fire pump or the release system for the fixed firefighting system
   - Relevant officers and crew lack awareness of the location, operation and coverage area of ventilation stops in the accommodation, engine room and other protected areas
   - Officers and crew unaware of the location of fire alarm indicators in the accommodation and in the engine room
   - Relevant officers and crew not aware of the location and operation of the fuel cut-off quick-closing valves for main engine and auxiliary engines

8.2 More Detailed Inspection for Operational Requirements

- Relevant officers and crew unaware of the operation of lifesaving equipment and how to effectively test such equipment
- Relevant officers and crew unfamiliar with the operation of equipment, or procedures, intended to prevent maritime pollution; or
- Evidence of unsafe operations that pose a risk to life and the environment.

Observation by Port State Control Officer must be directly related to compliance with Convention requirements. In relating the deficiency, it is critical to note that having the necessary equipment installed and operational does not provide a capability as required by Convention unless the vessel's master and crew are familiar with the operation of the equipment and associated procedures as required by STCW Section A-I/4.4. Examples of deficiencies and relevant convention references are shown below:

1. Engineer officer unable to demonstrate the operation of fuel oil valves provided in accordance with SOLAS regulation II-2/4.2.2.3.4 from outside the machinery space

   Note: This would be related to SOLAS regulation XI-1/4.

2. Engineer officer unable to demonstrate the operation of the sewage treatment plant required by regulation 2 of MARPOL Annex IV

   Note: This would be related to regulation 14 of MARPOL Annex IV.

   Note: Where the sewage treatment plant was found to be unserviceable, or sewage had been discharged into the sea this should also be related as evidence of the failure of operational requirements.

3. On a vessel subject to SOLAS regulation V/19.2.10 deck officer unable to demonstrate the process of planning and conducting a navigational passage and unable to demonstrate how to determine the vessel position using ECDIS

   Note: This could be related to SOLAS regulation XI-1/4, or section A-I/4.4 of STCW. Depending on the nature and scope of the issues could be used, noting SOLAS has a broader scope.

8.2.5 Detailed Guidance on Assessing Compliance with Operational Requirements

Detailed guidance on areas to be inspected is provided in part 2 of this chapter. Detailed guidance is divided into means of assessing compliance day to day activities and emergency preparedness. An assessment of compliance in respect of both should be undertaken where the circumstances warrant it. The Port State Control Officer should consider requesting a drill be conducted where vessel's records indicate that the specified drill has not been conducted in accordance with the Convention requirements.

8.2.6 Witnessing and Assessment of Drills

If a drill will involve passengers, it is prudent to provide as much notice as possible before the start of the drill to enable the vessel's master to inform the passengers about the drill. The information should be broadcast by public announcements in all relevant languages for the route concerned. The announcement should be repeated during the drill with appropriate intervals. The completion of the drill should be announced to the passengers. During the conduct of a drill, the Port State Control Officer should consider questioning the crew members, particularly those assigned to assist any passengers, to get an impression of the safety awareness on board the vessel. When witnessing a drill, the Port State Control Officer should seek:

1. Confirmation that the crew follow what is required of them by the muster list
2. Confirmation that there are sufficient personnel assigned to the various parties to cope with the duties given to them
3. Confirmation that there is an effective means of communication between the party, the party leader and the bridge, and that relevant information is being exchanged
4. Confirmation of the efficiency of the crew working as a team. This would be based on questioning of personnel and observation of their actions the response times should be noted of the various parties in assembling at their stations and the reaction of the parties to unplanned events should also be noted
5. Confirmation that core members of the crew can understand each other
6. Confirmation of the efficiency of the equipment used, for example:
   - that the fire alarms are audible and efficient
   - that the fire and watertight doors close as required
   - that items of personal firefighting equipment appear well maintained; and
7. Confirmation that the response time was considered fast enough (taking account of the safety of the drill) considering the size of the vessel and the locations of fire, personnel and firefighting equipment.

In the case of evacuation or abandon vessel drills:

1. Confirmation that the escape arrangements for passengers/crew from lower decks are adequate, that the assembly or muster stations are clearly indicated, that the crew are familiar with the layout of the vessel and can respond to changes in circumstances, for example directing passengers to avoid a smoke-filled area; and
2. Confirmation that the boat lowering party is proficient and that boats are lowered and ready for embarkation with ancillary equipment deployed.

If the Port State Control Officer determines that the crew are unfamiliar with their duties or incapable of safely operating the lifesaving and firefighting equipment, the Port State Control Officer should halt the drill, notify the vessel's master that the drill was unsuccessful and use their professional judgement to establish the next steps, noting the likelihood that this will establish "clear grounds" for a more detailed inspection. Having assessed the extent to which operational requirements are complied with, the Port State Control Officer should then exercise their professional judgement to determine whether the operational familiarity of the crew (as a whole) is of sufficient level to allow the vessel to sail without danger to the vessel or persons on board or presenting an unreasonable threat of harm to the marine environment.

8.2.7 Detention Under Operational Requirements

The Port State Control procedures identifies a substandard vessel as being one where operational safety is substantially below the standards required by the relevant convention and specifically, in the case of operational requirements, where there is

> insufficiency of operational proficiency, or unfamiliarity of essential operational procedures by the crew.

In such cases the relevant operational requirements provisions of conventions require the port State to take such action as necessary to bring vessels into compliance where it is found that the vessel's master and or crew are unfamiliar with essential shipboard procedures. The following provisions are relevant:

1. SOLAS regulation XI-1/4
2. MARPOL Annex I, regulation 11
3. MARPOL Annex II, regulation 16.9
4. MARPOL Annex III, regulation 9
5. MARPOL Annex IV, regulation 14
6. MARPOL Annex V, regulation 9
7. MARPOL Annex VI, regulation 10; and
8. STCW, Article X and regulation I/4 and section A-I/4.

8.3 Specific Inspection Activities

This section provides detailed guidance on specific inspection activities described in the previous section of this chapter with respect to the assessment of compliance with operation requirements in relation to day-to-day activities.

8.3.1 Bridge Operation

The Port State Control Officer may determine if officers in charge of a navigational watch are familiar with bridge control and navigational equipment, changing the steering mode from automatic to manual and vice versa, and the vessel's manoeuvring characteristics. All officers in charge of a navigational watch should have knowledge of the location and operation of all safety and navigational equipment. Moreover, the vessel's officer(s) should be familiar with procedures which apply to the navigation of the vessel in all circumstances and should be aware of all information available. The Port State Control Officer may also verify the familiarity of the vessel's officers with all the information available to them such as manoeuvring characteristics of the vessel, lifesaving signals, up to date nautical publications, checklists concerning bridge procedures, instructions and manuals. The Permit to Operate High-Speed Craft (HSC) includes limitations of the maximum significant wave height (and wind force for hovercraft) within which the craft may operate. When carrying out inspections of HSC, Port State Control Officers may verify by the logbook and the weather records whether these limitations have been respected. Port State Control Officers may find that a voyage had to be completed when worse weather conditions than permitted were encountered and not expected according to the weather forecast, but a new voyage should not commence in such conditions. The Port State Control Officers may verify the familiarity of the vessel's officers with procedures such as periodic tests and checks of equipment, preparations for arrival and departure, changeover of steering modes, signalling, communications, alarm system, manoeuvring, emergencies and logbook entries.

8.3.2 Cargo Operation

The Port State Control Officer may determine if vessel's personnel assigned to specific duties related to the cargo and cargo equipment are familiar with those duties, any dangers posed by the cargo and with the measures to be taken in such a context. This will require the availability of all relevant cargo information as required by SOLAS 1974 regulation VI/2. With respect to the carriage of solid bulk cargoes, the Port State Control Officer should verify, as appropriate, that cargo loading is performed in accordance with a vessel's loading plan and unloading in accordance with a vessel's unloading plan agreed by the vessel and the terminal, accounting for the information provided by the loading instrument, where fitted. The Port State Control Officer, when appropriate, may determine whether the responsible crew members are familiar with the relevant provisions of the International Maritime Solid Bulk Cargoes Code (IMSBC Code), particularly those concerning moisture limits and trimming of the cargo. Additionally, it is expected that the responsible crew members have appropriate knowledge of the recommendatory IMO Code of Safe Practice for Ships Carrying Timber Deck Cargoes (2011 TDC Code) and

8.3 Specific Inspection Activities

the Code of Safe Practice for Cargo Stowage and Securing (CSS Code) (non-mandatory, except mandatory Sect. 1.9), as amended. Some solid materials transported in bulk can present a hazard during transport because of their chemical nature or physical properties. Section 2 of the IMSBC Code gives general precautions. Section 4 of the IMSBC Code contains the obligation imposed on the shipper to provide all necessary information to ensure safe transport of the cargo. The Port State Control Officer may determine whether all relevant details, including all relevant certificates of tests, have been provided to the vessel's master by the shipper. For some cargoes, such as cargoes which are subject to liquefaction, special precautions are given (refer to section 7 of the IMSBC Code). The Port State Control Officer may determine whether all precautions are met with special attention to the stability of those vessels engaged in the transport of cargoes subject to liquefaction and solid hazardous waste in bulk. Officers responsible for cargo handling and operation and key crew members of oil tankers, chemical tankers and liquefied gas carriers should be familiar with the cargo and cargo equipment and with the safety measures as stipulated in the relevant sections of the IBC and IGC Codes. For the carriage of grain in bulk, reference is made to part C of chapter VI of SOLAS 1974 and the mandatory International Code for the Safe Carriage of Grain in Bulk (Grain Code). The Port State Control Officer may determine whether the operations and loading manuals include all the relevant information for safe loading and unloading operations in port as well as in transit conditions.

8.3.3 Operation of Machinery

The Port State Control Officer may determine if responsible vessel's personnel are familiar with their duties related to operating essential machinery, such as:

1. Emergency and standby sources of electrical power
2. Auxiliary steering gear
3. Bilge and fire pumps; and
4. Any other equipment essential in emergency situations.

The Port State Control Officer may verify whether the responsible vessel's personnel are familiar with, inter alia:

1. Emergency generator:
   - Actions which are necessary before the engine can be started
   - Different possibilities to start the engine in combination with the source of starting energy
   - Procedures when the first attempts to start the engine fail; and
2. Standby generator engine:
   - Possibilities to start the standby engine, automatic or by hand

- Blackout procedures; and
- Load-sharing system.

The Port State Control Officer may verify whether the responsible vessel's personnel are familiar with, inter alia:

1. Which type of auxiliary steering gear system applies to the vessel
2. How it is indicated which steering gear unit is in operation; and
3. What action is needed to bring the auxiliary steering gear into operation.

The Port State Control Officer may verify whether the responsible vessel's personnel are familiar with, inter alia:

4. Bilge pumps:
   - Number and location of bilge pumps installed on board the vessel (including emergency bilge pumps)
   - Starting procedures for all these bilge pumps
   - Appropriate valves to operate; and
   - Most likely causes of failure of bilge pump operation and their possible remedies; and
5. Fire pumps:
   - Number and location of fire pumps installed on board the vessel (including the emergency fire pump)
   - Starting procedures for all these pumps; and
   - Appropriate valves to operate.

The Port State Control Officer may verify whether the responsible vessel's personnel are familiar with, inter alia:

1. Starting and maintenance of lifeboat engine and or rescue boat engine
2. Local control procedures for those systems which are normally controlled from the navigating bridge
3. Use of the emergency and fully independent sources of electrical power of radio installations
4. Maintenance procedures for batteries
5. Emergency stops, fire detection system and alarm system operation of watertight and fire doors (stored energy systems); and
6. Change of control from automatic to manual for cooling water and lube oil systems for main and auxiliary engines.

8.3.4 Manuals, Instructions, etc.

The Port State Control Officer may determine if the appropriate crew members are able to understand the information given in manuals, instructions, etc. relevant to the safe condition and operation of the vessel and its equipment, and if they are aware of the requirements for maintenance, periodic testing, training, drills and recording of logbook entries. The following information, inter alia, should be provided on board and Port State Control Officer may determine whether it is in a language or languages understood by the crew and whether crew members concerned are aware of the contents and are able to respond accordingly:

1. Instructions concerning the maintenance and operation of all the equipment and installations on board for the fighting and containment of fire should be kept under one cover, readily available in an accessible position
2. Clear instructions to be followed in the event of an emergency should be provided for every person on board
3. Illustrations and instructions in appropriate languages should be posted in passenger cabins and be conspicuously displayed at muster stations and other passenger spaces to inform passengers of their muster station, the essential action they must take in an emergency and the method of donning lifejackets
4. Posters and signs should be provided on or in the vicinity of survival craft and their launching controls and shall illustrate the purpose of controls and the procedures for operating the appliance and give relevant instructions or warnings
5. Instructions for onboard maintenance of lifesaving appliances
6. Training manuals should be provided in each crew mess room and recreation room or in each crew cabin; the training manual, which may comprise several volumes, should contain instructions and information, in easily understood terms illustrated wherever possible, on the life-saving appliances provided in the vessel and on the best method of survival; and
7. SOPEP in accordance with regulation 37 of MARPOL Annex I, or SMPEP for noxious liquid substances in accordance with regulation 17 of MARPOL Annex II, where applicable; and 8 stability booklet, associated stability plans, stability information and approved stability instrument for tankers.

8.3.5 Oil and Oily Mixtures from Machinery Spaces

The Port State Control Officer may determine if all operational requirements of MARPOL Annex I have been met, considering:

1. The quantity of oil residues generated
2. The capacity of the sludge and bilge water holding tank; and
3. The capacity of the oily-water separator.

An inspection of the Oil Record Book should be made. The Port State Control Officer may determine if reception facilities have been used and note any alleged inadequacy of such facilities. The Port State Control Officer may determine whether the responsible officer is familiar with the handling of sludge and bilge water. The relevant items from the guidelines for systems for handling oily wastes in machinery spaces of vessels may be used as guidance. Accounting for the above, the Port State Control Officer may determine if the ullage of the sludge tank is sufficient for the expected generated sludge during the next intended voyage. The Port State Control Officer may verify that, in respect of vessels for which the Administration has waived the requirements of regulations 14(1) and (2) of MARPOL Annex I, all oily bilge water is retained on board for subsequent discharge to a reception facility. When reception facilities in other ports have not been used because of inadequacy, the Port State Control Officer should advise the vessel's master to report the inadequacy of the reception facility to the vessel's Flag State, in conformity with the Format for reporting alleged inadequacies of port reception facilities (MEPC.1/Circ.834/Rev.1, appendix 1 of the annex), as may be amended.

8.3.6 Loading, Unloading and Cleaning Procedures for Cargo Spaces of Tankers

The Port State Control Officer may determine if all operational requirements of MARPOL Annexes I or II have been met, accounting for the type of tanker and the type of cargo carried, including the inspection of the Oil Record Book and or Cargo Record Book. The Port State Control Officer may determine if the reception facilities have been used and note any alleged inadequacy of such facilities. For the control on loading, unloading and cleaning procedures for tankers carrying oil, reference may be made to Chap. 6 where guidance is given for the inspection of crude oil washing operations. In Chap. 5, the Port State Control Officer will find detailed guidelines for in-port inspection of crude oil washing procedures. For the control on loading, unloading and cleaning procedures for tankers carrying noxious liquid substances, reference may be made to Chap. 6 where guidance is given for the inspection of unloading, stripping and prewash operations. More detailed guidelines for these inspections are given in Chap. 5. When reception facilities in other ports have not been used because of inadequacy, the Port State Control Officer should advise the vessel's master to report the inadequacy of the reception facility to the vessel's Flag State, in conformity with MEPC.1/Circ.834/Rev.1, as may be amended. The Garbage Record Book may be presented in an electronic format. A declaration from the Administration should be viewed to accept this electronic record book. If a declaration cannot be provided, a hard copy record book will need to be presented for examination. When a vessel is permitted to proceed to the next port with residues of noxious liquid substances on board in excess of those permitted to be discharged into the sea during the vessel's passage, it should be ascertained that the residues can be received by that port. At the same time, that port should be informed, if practicable.

8.3.7 Dangerous Goods and Harmful Substances in Packaged Form

The Port State Control Officer may determine if the required shipping documents for the carriage of dangerous goods and harmful substances carried in packaged form are provided on board and whether the dangerous goods and harmful substances are properly stowed and segregated, and the crew members are familiar with the essential action to be taken in an emergency involving such packaged cargo (see SOLAS 1974 regulation VII/3). Vessel types and cargo spaces of vessels of over 500 gross tonnages built on or after 1 September 1984 and vessel types and cargo spaces of vessels of less than 500 gross tonnage built on or after 1 February 1992 are to fully comply with the requirements of SOLAS 1974 chapter II-2. Administrations may reduce the requirements for cargo vessels of less than 500 gross tonnage, but such reductions shall be recorded in the Document of Compliance. A Document of Compliance is not required for vessels which only carry class 6.2, class 7 or dangerous goods in limited quantities and excepted quantities. MARPOL Annex III contains requirements for the carriage of harmful substances in packaged form which are identified in the IMDG Code as marine pollutants. Cargoes which are determined to be marine pollutants should be labelled and stowed in accordance with MARPOL Annex III. The Port State Control Officer may determine whether a Document of Compliance is on board and whether the vessel's personnel are familiar with this document provided by the Administration as evidence of compliance of construction and equipment with the requirements. Additional control may consist of:

1. Checking whether the dangerous goods have been stowed on board in conformity with the Document of Compliance, using the dangerous goods manifest or the stowage plan, required by SOLAS 1974 chapter VII; this manifest or stowage plan may be combined with the one required under MARPOL Annex III
2. Checking whether inadvertent pumping of leaking flammable or toxic liquids is not possible in case these substances are carried in under-deck cargo spaces; or
3. Determining whether the vessel's personnel are familiar with the relevant provisions of the Medical First Aid Guide and Emergency Procedures for Ships Carrying Dangerous Goods.

8.3.8 Garbage

The Port State Control Officer may determine if all operational requirements of MARPOL Annex V have been met. The Port State Control Officer may determine if the reception facilities have been used and note any alleged inadequacy of such facilities. The 2017 Guidelines for the implementation of MARPOL Annex V (resolution MEPC.295(71)), as may be amended, are to assist vessel operators complying with the requirements set forth in Annex V and domestic laws. The Port State Control Officer may determine whether:

1. Vessel's personnel are aware of the guidance pertaining to the management of shipboard garbage, and in particular section 2 on "Garbage management"; and
2. Vessel's personnel are familiar with the disposal and discharge requirements under MARPOL Annex V inside and outside a special area and are aware of the areas determined as special areas under MARPOL Annex V.

When reception facilities in other ports have not been used because of inadequacy, the Port State Control Officer should advise the vessel's master to report the inadequacy of the reception facility to the vessel's Flag State, in conformity with MEPC.1/Circ.834/Rev.1, as may be amended.

8.3.9 Sewage

The Port State Control Officer may determine:

1. If all operational requirements of MARPOL Annex IV have been met; the Port State Control Officer may determine if the sewage treatment system, comminuting and disinfecting system or holding tank has been used and note any alleged inadequacy of the system or holding tank; and
2. That appropriate vessel's personnel are familiar with the correct operation of the sewage treatment system, comminuting and disinfecting system or holding tank.

The Port State Control Officer may determine whether appropriate vessel's personnel are familiar with the discharge requirements of regulation 11 of MARPOL Annex IV. When reception facilities in other ports have not been used because of inadequacy, the Port State Control Officer should advise the vessel's master to report the inadequacy of the reception facility to the vessel's Flag State, in conformity with the waste reception facility reporting requirements (MEPC.1/Circ.834/Rev.1, as may be amended).

8.3.10 Air Pollution Prevention

The Port State Control Officer may determine whether:

1. The vessel's master or crew are familiar with the procedures to prevent emissions of ozone-depleting substances and sulphur when equivalent arrangements are in place
2. The vessel's master or crew are familiar with the proper operation and maintenance of diesel engines, in accordance with their Technical Files
3. The vessel's master or crew have undertaken the necessary fuel changeover procedures or equivalent, associated with demonstrating compliance within a SO_x emission control area
4. The vessel's master or crew are familiar with the garbage screening procedure to ensure that prohibited garbage is not incinerated
5. The vessel's master or crew are familiar with the operation of the shipboard incinerator, as required by regulation 16.2 of MARPOL Annex VI, within the limit provided in appendix IV to the Annex, in accordance with the operational manual
6. The vessel's master or crew recognises the regulation of emissions of volatile organic compounds (VOCs), when the vessel is in ports or terminals under the jurisdiction of a Party to the 1997 Protocol to MARPOL in which VOCs emissions are to be regulated, and is familiar with the proper operation of a vapour collection system approved by the Administration (in case the vessel is a tanker as defined in regulation 2.27 of MARPOL Annex VI); and
7. The vessel's master or crew are familiar with bunker delivery procedures in respect of bunker delivery notes (BDN) and retained samples as required by regulation 18 of MARPOL Annex VI.

8.4 Specific Guidance

This section provides detailed guidance on specific inspection activities described in part 1 of this chapter with respect to the assessment of preparedness for emergencies and drills.

8.4.1 Muster List

The Port State Control Officer may determine if the crew members are aware of their duties indicated in the muster list and that they are familiar with the duties assigned to them and are aware of the locations where they should perform their duties, this is done by asking the crew relevant questions. This could be done prior to the drill or during the drill, for instance questioning of stairway guides on a passenger vessel. To determine whether the muster list is up to date, the Port State Control Officer may require an up-to-date crew list. The Port State Control Officer may ensure that muster lists are exhibited in conspicuous places throughout the vessel, including the navigational bridge, the engine room and the crew accommodation spaces. When determining if the muster list is in accordance with the regulations, the Port State Control Officer may verify whether:

1. The muster list shows the duties assigned to the different members of the crew
2. The muster list specifies which officers are assigned to ensure that lifesaving and fire appliances are maintained in good condition and are ready for immediate use
3. The muster list specifies the substitutes for key persons who may become disabled, considering that different emergencies may call for different actions
4. The muster list shows the duties assigned to crew members in relation to passengers in case of emergency; and
5. The format of the muster list used on passenger vessels is approved and is drawn up in the language or languages required by the vessel's Flag State and in the English language.

To determine whether the muster list is up to date, the Port State Control Officer may require an up-to-date crew list, if available, to verify this. The Port State Control Officer may determine whether the duties assigned to crew members manning the survival craft (lifeboats or life rafts) are in accordance with the regulations and verify that a deck officer or certificated person is placed in charge of each survival craft to be used. However, the Administration (of the Flag State), having due regard to the nature of the voyage, the number of persons on board and the characteristics of the vessel, may permit persons practised in the handling and operation of life rafts to be placed in charge of life rafts in lieu of persons qualified as above. A second-in-command shall also be nominated in the case of lifeboats. Every motorised survival craft shall have a person assigned who can operate the engine and carrying out minor adjustments.

8.4.2 Communication During Drills

The Port State Control Officer may determine if the key crew members are able to communicate with each other, and with passengers, as appropriate, in such a way that the safe operation of the vessel is not impaired, especially in emergency situations. For drills, key crew members could be but are not limited to:

1. Bridge team including GMDSS operators who must also be able to communicate with the shore and other vessels
2. Fire parties
3. Damage control parties

8.4 Specific Guidance

4. Boat preparation parties; or
5. Passenger muster personnel on passenger vessels.

The Port State Control Officer should verify the working language of the vessel. The crew members assigned to assist passengers should be able to give the necessary information to the passengers in case of an emergency. The Port State Control Officer should determine, if UHF or VHF handheld radios are being used for drills, that the crew are familiar with the equipment, that they are aware of reception dead zones/areas and what alternative communication methods are available. When drills are being conducted the Port State Control Officer should establish that there are sufficient personnel on the bridge to make decisions, navigate the vessel as necessary and deal with the considerable amount of communication that is likely. When a vessel is in difficulty it is likely that shore-based organisations, such as the operator of the vessel and regional rescue coordination centres, will need to be involved. The Port State Control Officer should confirm the vessel's master and crew are aware of procedures where shore-based communication is required and how such communication can be established.

8.4.3 Search and Rescue Plan

For passenger vessels, the Port State Control Officer may verify that there is on board an approved plan for cooperation with appropriate search and rescue services in the event of an emergency.

8.4.4 Fire and Abandon Ship Drills

The Port State Control Officer witnessing a fire and abandon ship drill should ensure that the crew members are familiar with their duties and the proper use of the vessel's installations and equipment. When setting a drill scenario, witnessing the drill and finally assessing the standard of the drill, it is important to emphasise that the Port State Control Officer is not looking for an exceptional drill, particularly on cargo vessels. The main points for the Port State Control Officer to be satisfied are:

1. In the event of a shipboard emergency can the crew organise themselves into an effective team to tackle the emergency.
2. Can the crew communicate effectively?
3. Is the vessel's master in control and is information flowing to/from the command centre?
4. In the event of the situation getting out of hand can the crew safely abandon the vessel.

It is important that when setting the scenario, the Port State Control Officer clearly explains to the vessel's master exactly what is required and expected during the drill, bearing in mind there may be language difficulties. Port State Control Officers should not be intimidating, not interfere during the drill nor offer advice. The Port State Control Officer should stand back and observe only, making appropriate notes. It is important to emphasise that the Port State Control Officer's role is not to teach or train but to bear witness. Drills should be carried out at a safe speed. Port State Control Officers should not expect to see operational drills conducted in real time. During drills, care should be taken to ensure that everybody familiarises themself with their duties and with the equipment. If necessary, drills should be stopped if the Port State Control Officer considers that the crew are carrying out unsafe practices or if there is a real emergency.

8.4.5 Fire Drills

The Port State Control Officer may witness a fire drill carried out by the crew assigned to these duties on the muster list. After consultation with the master of the vessel, one or more specific locations of the vessel may be selected for a simulated fire. A crew member may be sent to the location(s) and activate a fire alarm system or use other means to give the alarm. At the location the Port State Control Officer can describe the fire indication to the crew member and observe how the report of fire is relayed to the bridge or damage control centre. At this point most vessels will sound the crew alarm to summon the firefighting parties to their stations. The Port State Control Officer should observe the firefighting party arriving on the scene, breaking out their equipment and fighting the simulated fire. Team leaders should be giving orders as appropriate to their crews and passing the word back to the bridge or damage control centre on the conditions. The firefighting crews should be observed for proper donning and use of their equipment. The Port State Control Officer should make sure that all the gear is complete. Merely mustering the crew with their gear is not acceptable. Crew response to personnel injuries can be checked by selecting a crew member as a simulated casualty. The Port State Control Officer should observe how the word is passed and the response of stretcher and medical teams. Handling a stretcher properly through narrow passageways, doors and stairways is difficult and takes practice. The drill should, as far as practicable, be conducted as if there were an actual emergency. Those crew members assigned to other duties related to a fire drill, such as the manning of the emergency generators, the CO_2 room, the sprinkler and emergency fire pumps, should also be involved in the drill. The Port State Control Officer may ask these crew members to explain their duties and, if possible, to demonstrate their familiarity. On passenger vessels, special attention should be paid to the duties of those crew members assigned to the closing of manually operated doors and fire dampers. These closing devices should be operated by the responsible persons in the areas of the simulated fire(s) during the drill. Crew members not assigned to the firefighting teams are generally assigned to locations throughout the passenger accommodations to assist in passenger evacuation. These crew members should be asked to explain their duties and the meaning of the various emergency signals and asked to point out the two means of escape from the area, and where the passengers are to report. Crew members assigned to assist passengers should be able to communicate at least enough information to direct a passenger to the proper muster and embarkation stations.

8.4.6 Abandon Ship Drills

After consultation with the vessel's master, the Port State Control Officer may require an abandon ship drill for one or more survival craft. The essence of this drill is that the survival craft are manned and operated by the crew members assigned to them on the muster list. If possible, the Port State Control Officer should include the rescue boat(s) in this drill. SOLAS 1974 chapter III gives specific requirements on abandon ship training and drills, of which the following principles are particularly relevant. The drill should, as far as practicable, be conducted as if there were an actual emergency. The abandon ship drill should include:

1. Summoning crew, and passengers where applicable, to the muster station(s) with the required alarm and ensuring that they are aware of the order to abandon the vessel as specified in the muster list
2. Reporting to the stations and preparing for the duties described in the muster list
3. Checking that crew, and passengers where applicable, are suitably dressed
4. Checking that lifejackets are correctly donned
5. Lowering at least one lifeboat after the necessary preparation for launching
6. Starting and operating the lifeboat engine
7. Operating the davits used for launching life rafts
8. Conducting a mock search and rescue of passenger trapped in their staterooms (if applicable)
9. Giving instructions in the use of radio lifesaving appliances
10. Testing emergency lighting and low location lights if applicable for mustering and abandonment; and
11. If the vessel is fitted with marine evacuation systems, exercising the procedures required for the deployment of such systems up to the point immediately preceding actual deployment.

If the lifeboat lowered during the drill is not the rescue boat, the rescue boat should be lowered as well, taking account that it is boarded and launched in the shortest possible time. The Port State Control Officer should ensure that crew members are familiar with the duties assigned to them during abandon vessel operations and that the crew member in charge of the survival craft has complete knowledge of the operation and equipment of the survival craft. Care needs to be taken when requiring a vessel to lower lifeboats. The number of persons inside the lifeboats during launching for the purpose of a drill should be at the vessel's master's discretion, noting that SOLAS 1974 does not require persons in the lifeboat during lowering and recovery. The purpose of this is to reduce the risk of accidents during launching and recovery; however, this must be balanced out with the risk of embarking and or disembarking while the boat is still in the water, if the boat is to be taken away and run. Each survival craft should be stowed in a state of continuous readiness so that two crew members can carry out preparations for embarking and launching in less than five minutes.

8.4.7 Enclosed Space Entry and Rescue Drills

After consultation with the vessel's master, the Port State Control Officer may require an enclosed space entry and rescue drill. The essence of this drill is to confirm that crew members are familiar with the procedure to enter an enclosed space and to rescue personnel safely, can demonstrate an enclosed space entry and rescue drill, and can communicate effectively when entering an enclosed space in case of planned entry and or an emergency. The place of the drill can be selected at an assumed enclosed space; it is not necessary to select an actual enclosed space. The Port State Control Officer should check the structure of the enclosed space, the scenarios of the drills and the responsible officers listed on the muster list where applicable. The enclosed space entry and rescue drill should include:

1. Checking and use of personal protective equipment required for entry
2. Checking and use of communication equipment and procedures
3. Checking and use of instruments for measuring the atmosphere in enclosed spaces
4. Checking and use of rescue equipment and procedures; and
5. Instructions in first aid and resuscitation techniques.

8.4.8 Emergency Steering Drills

After consultation with the vessel's master, the Port State Control Officer may require an emergency steering drill. The essence of this drill is to confirm crew members are familiar with the procedure for emergency steering. The Port State Control Officer may check the procedure and means of communication at both the navigation bridge and the steering gear room. The emergency steering drills should include:

1. Direct control within the steering gear compartment
2. Communication procedure with the navigational bridge; and
3. Operation of alternative power supplies where applicable.

8.4.9 Damage Control Plan and Shipboard Oil Pollution Emergency Plan (SOPEP) or Shipboard Marine Pollution Emergency Plan (SMPEP)

The Port State Control Officer may determine if a damage control plan is provided on a passenger vessel and whether the crew members are familiar with their duties and the proper use of the vessel's installations and equipment for damage control purposes. The same applies with respect to SOPEPs on all vessels and SMPEPs where applicable. The Port State Control Officer may determine if the officers of the vessel are aware of the contents of the damage control booklet, which should be available to them, or of the damage control plan. The officers may be asked to explain the action to be taken in various damage conditions. The officers may also be asked to explain about the boundaries of the watertight compartments, the openings therein with the means of closure and position of any controls thereof and the arrangements for the correction of any list due to flooding. The officers should have a sound knowledge of the effect of trim and stability of their vessel in the event of damage to and consequent flooding of a compartment and countermeasures to be taken.

8.4.10 Fire Control Plan

The Port State Control Officer may determine if a fire control plan or booklet is provided, whether the crew members are familiar with the information given in the fire control plan or booklet, and whether, for tankers, crew members are familiar with the approved stability instrument. The Port State Control Officer may verify that fire control plans are permanently exhibited for the guidance of the vessel's officers. Alternatively, booklets containing the information about the fire control plan may be supplied to each officer, and one copy should always be available on board in an accessible position. Plans and booklets should be kept up to date, any alterations being recorded therein as soon as possible. The Port State Control Officer may determine that the responsible officers, especially those who are assigned to related duties on the muster list, are aware of the information provided by the fire control plan or booklet and how to act in case of a fire. The Port State Control Officer may ensure that the officers in charge of the vessel are familiar with the principal structural members which form part of the various fire sections and the means of access to the different compartments.

ISM Code

The International Safety Management Code (ISM Code) was adopted by the IMO Assembly at its eighteenth session by resolution A.741(18) and was amended by resolutions MSC.104(73), MSC.179(79), MSC.195(80), MSC.273(85) and MSC.353(92). The ISM Code has been made mandatory through SOLAS 1974 regulation IX/3. The Administration is responsible for verifying compliance with the requirements of the ISM Code and issuing Documents of Compliance to companies and Safety Management Certificates to vessels. This verification is carried out by the Administration, or a RO. Port State Control Officers do not perform safety management audits. ISM auditing is the responsibility of the Flag State and the company and does not fall under the scope of Port State control. Port State Control Officers conduct inspections of vessels, which are a sampling process and give a snapshot of the vessel on a particular day. The SMS documentation is in the vessel's working language, which may not be understood by the Port State Control Officer. The procedure may not be harmonised if the Port State Control Officer is only able to review the SMS documentation on those vessels where they can understand the language. To this end, the IMO has produced guidance for Port State Control Officers for the harmonised application of related technical or operational deficiencies found in relation to the ISM Code during a Port State Control inspection.

The ISM Code applies to the following types of vessels engaged in international voyages:

1. All passenger vessels including passenger high-speed craft
2. Oil tankers, chemical tankers, gas carriers, bulk carriers and cargo high-speed craft of 500 gross tonnage and above; and

3. Other cargo vessels and self-propelled mobile offshore drilling units (MODUs) of 500 gross tonnage and above.

For establishing the applicability SOLAS 1974 chapter IX and the ISM Code, "gross tonnage" refers to the gross tonnage of the vessel as determined under the provisions of TONNAGE 1969, and as stated on the International Tonnage Certificate of the vessel. The ISM Code does not apply to government-operated vessels used for non-commercial purposes.

9.1 Relevant Documentation

The relevant documentation which relates to the application of the ISM Code are as follows:

1. SOLAS 1974
2. ISM Code
3. Copy of the Interim DOC or copy of the DOC
4. Interim SMC or SMC; and
5. MSC/Circ.1059-MEPC/Circ.401, as may be amended.

9.2 Definitions and Abbreviations

SOLAS:	International Convention for the Safety of Life at Sea, 1974, as amended
ISM Code:	International Safety Management Code
	"*The International Management Code for the Safe Operation of Ships and for Pollution Prevention*", as adopted by resolution A.741(18), as amended
Procedures for	*Procedures for Port State Control, 2021*, as adopted by resolution A.1155(32), as may be amended
Company:	The owner of the vessel or any other organisation or person such as the manager, or the bareboat charterer, who has assumed the responsibility for operation of the vessel from the shipowner and who, on assuming such responsibility, has agreed to take over all duties and responsibility imposed by the Code
Administration:	The Government of the State whose Flag the vessel is entitled to fly
DOC:	Document of Compliance
	A document issued to a company which complies with the requirements of the ISM Code

SMC:	Safety Management Certificate
	A document issued to a vessel which signifies that the company and its shipboard management operate in accordance with the approved safety management system
SMS:	Safety management system
	A structured and documented system enabling company personnel to effectively implement the company safety and environmental protection policy
Objective:	Quantitative or qualitative information, records or statements of fact.
Evidence:	Fact pertaining to safety or to the existence and implementation of a safety management system element, which is based on observation, measurement or test and which can be verified
Valid certificate:	A certificate that has been issued, electronically or on paper, directly by a Party to a relevant convention or on its behalf by a recognised organisation, and contains accurate and effective dates, meets the provisions of the relevant convention, and with which the particulars of the vessel, its crew and its equipment correspond
PSC:	Port State Control
PSCO:	Port State Control Officer
RO:	Recognised organisation
	An organisation recognised by the Administration
MODU:	Mobile offshore drilling unit
ISM-related:	A technical and/or operational deficiency which has been assessed by the Port State Control Officer to be objective evidence of a failure, or lack of effectiveness, of the implementation of the ISM Code, and which is marked as "ISM-related" in the inspection report
ISM deficiency:	A deficiency that is cited against the ISM Code.

9.3 Inspection of Vessel

9.3.1 Initial Inspection

Initial inspection should be carried out in accordance with the Procedures for Port State Control. During the initial Port State Control inspection, the Port State Control Officer should verify that the vessel carries the ISM certificates according to the provisions of chapter IX of SOLAS 1974 and the ISM Code by examining the copy of the DOC and the SMC, for which the following points are to be considered:

1. A copy of the DOC should be on board. However, according to the provisions of SOLAS 1974, the copy of the DOC is not required to be authenticated or certified. The copy of the DOC should have the required endorsements.
2. The SMC is not valid unless the operating company holds a valid DOC for that vessel type. The vessel type in the SMC should be included in the DOC and the company's particulars should be the same on both the DOC and the SMC. The SMC should have the required endorsements.
3. The validity of an Interim DOC should not exceed a period of 12 months. The validity of an Interim SMC should not exceed a period of six months. In special cases, the Administration, or at the request of the Administration another Government, may extend the validity of the Interim SMC for a period which should not exceed six months from the date of expiry.
4. ROs may issue a short-term DOC or SMC not exceeding five months, while the full-term certificate is being prepared in accordance with their internal procedures. If a renewal verification has been completed and a new SMC cannot be issued or placed on board the vessel before the expiry date of the existing certificate, the Administration or RO may endorse the existing certificate. Such a certificate should be accepted as valid for a further period which should not exceed five months from the expiry date.
5. If a vessel at the time when an SMC expires is not in a port in which SMC verification is to be carried out, the Administration may extend the period of validity of the SMC but this extension should be granted only for the purpose of allowing the vessel to complete its voyage to the port in which SMC verification is to be carried out, and then only in cases where it appears proper and reasonable to do so.
6. No SMC should be extended for a period of longer than three months, and the vessel to which an extension is granted should not, on its arrival in the port in which SMC verification is to be carried out, be entitled by virtue of such extension to leave that port without having a new SMC. When the renewal verification is completed, the new SMC should be valid until a date not exceeding five years from the expiry date of the existing SMC before the extension was granted.
7. If no technical or operational-related deficiencies are found during an initial inspection carried out in accordance with the *Procedures for Port State Control and Guidelines*, there is no need to consider the ISM aspect.

9.3.2 Clear Grounds

Since the Port State Control Officer is not carrying out a safety management audit of the SMS during a Port State Control inspection, the term "clear grounds" is not applicable in this context. Clear grounds and the subsequent more detailed inspection only exist for technical or operational deficiencies.

9.3.3 More Detailed Inspection

If a more detailed inspection for technical or operational-related deficiencies is carried out, this should be done in accordance with the Procedures for port State control. Any technical and/or operational deficiencies found during this inspection should be individually or collectively considered by the Port State Control Officer, using their professional judgement, to indicate that either:

1. These do not show a failure, or lack of effectiveness, of the implementation of the ISM Code; or
2. There is a failure, or lack of effectiveness, of the implementation of the ISM Code.

If an outstanding ISM-related deficiency from a previous Port State Control inspection exists and the current Port State Control inspection is more than three months later, the Port State Control Officer will verify, during the present Port State Control inspection, the effectiveness of any corrective action taken by the company by examining the areas of the technical and/or operational deficiencies of the previous Port State Control inspection report which led to the issuance of the ISM deficiency.

9.4 Follow-Up Action

9.4.1 Technical, Operational and ISM Code Deficiencies

The principles outlined in the *Procedures for Port State Control* with respect to reporting and rectification of technical or operational deficiencies, and detention and release of the vessel are applicable. If there are technical or operational deficiencies reported:

1. Which, whether detainable or non-detainable, do not show a failure, or lack of effectiveness, of the implementation of the ISM Code, no ISM deficiency should be reported in the Port State Control inspection report
2. Of which at least one non-detainable deficiency indicates a failure, or lack of effectiveness, of the implementation of the ISM Code, a non-detainable ISM deficiency will be reported in the Port State Control inspection report with the requirement of corrective action within three months
3. Which individually do not lead to a detention but collectively warrant the detention of the vessel indicating a serious failure, or lack of effectiveness, of the implementation of the ISM Code, ISM deficiency will be reported in the Port State Control inspection report with the requirement that a safety management audit has to be carried out by the Administration or the RO before the vessel may be released from its detention; and

4. Of which at least one detainable deficiency indicates a serious failure, or lack of effectiveness, of the implementation of the ISM Code, a detainable ISM deficiency will be reported in the Port State Control inspection report with the requirement that a safety management audit has to be carried out by the Administration or the RO before the vessel may be released from detention.

Note: Where the Port State Control Officer considers that one or more technical and/or operational deficiencies are related to the ISM Code, this should be recorded as only one ISM deficiency.

The Port State Control Officer will verify the effectiveness of any corrective action as described in the section below. If examination of the areas in relation to an ISM deficiency with the requirement corrective action within three months is found not satisfactory, a new detainable ISM deficiency with the requirement that a safety management audit must be carried out by the Administration or the RO will be raised. In this case the Port State Control Officer should apply the following procedure:

1. Record one or more technical/operational deficiencies, detainable or not, in the same area(s) which led to the issuance of the previous ISM deficiency
2. Mark the deficiency or deficiencies "ISM-related" and add in the additional comments the following text: "This deficiency shows non-effective implementation of the ISM Code in the areas where the ISM deficiency or deficiencies were found during the Port State Control inspection on […]"; and
3. Record a new detainable ISM deficiency with the requirement that a safety management audit must be conducted by the Administration or the RO before the vessel may be released from detention.

9.4.2 Deficiencies not Warranting Detention

Minor typing errors in the DOC, the Interim DOC, the SMC, or Interim SMC should be recorded in the PSC inspection report as a technical deficiency with the certificates and no ISM deficiency should be recorded.

9.4.3 Deficiencies Warranting Detention

The following are deficiencies which may warrant detention:

1. Deficiencies of a technical and/or operational nature which individually or collectively provide objective evidence of a serious failure, or lack of effectiveness, of the implementation of the ISM Code

2. There is no SMC, Interim SMC and/or copy of the DOC or Interim DOC on board the vessel
3. There is no valid SMC or Interim SMC on board
4. The SMC intermediate verification is overdue
5. The SMC has expired and there is no objective evidence of an extension issued by the Administration; or the SMC has been withdrawn by the Administration
6. The DOC or Interim DOC has expired or been withdrawn
7. The vessel type as indicated on the SMC or Interim SMC is not listed on the DOC or Interim DOC
8. Evidence of the DOC annual verification is not available on board
9. The certificate number on the copy of the DOC and the endorsement pages are not the same; and
10. The company name, the company address or the issuing Government authority on the DOC or Interim DOC is not the same as on the SMC or Interim SMC.

9.5 Reporting

9.5.1 Technical and Operational-Related Deficiencies

All technical and/or operational deficiencies should be recorded as an individual deficiency in the Post State Control inspection report according to the *Procedures for Port State Control*. A technical deficiency with the defective item DOC/SMC or Interim DOC/SMC should be recorded in the Port State Control inspection report under the deficiency code addressing the DOC or SMC respectively.

9.5.2 ISM Deficiency

Where the Port State Control Officer has considered the technical and/or operational deficiencies found and concluded these provide objective evidence of a failure, serious failure or lack of effectiveness of the implementation of the ISM Code, an ISM deficiency should be recorded in the Port State Control inspection report.

Port State Control Procedures Related to LRIT

10

This chapter is intended to provide basic guidance to Port State Control Officers to verify compliance with the requirements of SOLAS 1974 for Long-Range Identification and Tracking (LRIT). LRIT equipment is required by the provisions of SOLAS 1974 regulation V/19-1, and the Revised performance standards and functional requirements for the Long-Range Identification and Tracking of Ships (resolution MSC.263(84)), as amended, and requires all passenger vessels, cargo vessels (including high-speed craft) over 300 gross tonnage and mobile offshore drilling units (MODUs) to send LRIT position information at least every six hours. Vessels fitted with an automatic identification system (AIS) and operated exclusively within sea area A1 are not required to comply with LRIT. Sea area A1 is defined by SOLAS 1974 regulation IV/2.1.12 as "an area within the radiotelephone coverage of at least one VHF coast station in which continuous DSC alerting is available, as may be defined by a Contracting Government". SOLAS Contracting Governments are expected to maintain an LRIT data centre, either on a national basis, or on a regional or cooperative basis with other Flag States and notify IMO of it. In turn, these LRIT data centres will forward, upon request, LRIT information from vessels entitled to fly their Flags, to other SOLAS Contracting Governments through the International LRIT Data Exchange. Port States are entitled to request LRIT information from foreign vessels that have indicated their intention to enter a port, port facility or place under its jurisdiction. In most cases a stand-alone Inmarsat C or Inmarsat mini-C terminal used for GMDSS, or vessel security alert system will function as the LRIT terminal, but other equipment may be employed for the LRIT function (example, Inmarsat D+ or Iridium).

10.1 Inspection of Vessels Required to Carry LRIT Equipment

10.1.1 Initial Inspection

The Port State Control Officer should first establish the sea area the vessel is certified to operate in. This verification should ensure that the vessel is subject to the LRIT regulation in relation to its vessel type and tonnage. After the certificate check, the Port State Control Officer should verify that:

1. The Record of Equipment (Form E, P or C) indicates LRIT as required, if applicable[1]; and
2. The equipment identified by the vessel's representative as the designated LRIT terminal is switched on.[2]

In case of recent transfer of Flag, the Port State Control Officer may further ensure that:

1. A conformance test report has been re-issued if the new Flag State does not recognise the issuing body of the existing conformance test report; or
2. A new conformance test has been carried out by the application service provider (ASP) on behalf of the Administration before issuance of a new test report and certificate.

10.1.2 Clear Grounds

Conditions which may warrant a more detailed inspection of equipment used for LRIT may comprise the following:

1. Defective main or emergency source of energy
2. Information or indication that LRIT equipment is not functioning properly
3. Vessel does not hold conformance test report; and
4. The "record of navigational activities" indicates that the LRIT installation has been switched off and that this has not been reported to the Flag Administration as required by SOLAS 1974 regulation V/19-1.7.2.

---

[1] A Record of Equipment is required for cargo vessels greater than 500 gross tonnage and passenger vessels.

[2] In exceptional circumstances and for the shortest duration possible, LRIT is capable of being switched off or may transmit less frequently (SOLAS 1974 regulation V/19-1.7.2 and resolution MSC.263(84), para 4.4.1).

10.1.3 More Detailed Inspection

In case of doubt or reports of malfunctioning of the LRIT installation, the Flag Administration may be contacted to determine if the vessel's LRIT information has been reliably relayed to the LRIT data centre. If any issues are identified at the initial inspection, a more detailed inspection of equipment used for LRIT may comprise the following:

1. Verification of the power supply, which should be connected to the main source of energy and the emergency source of energy—there is no requirement for an uninterrupted power source; if LRIT is part of the GMDSS radio-installation, the power supply should conform to GMDSS regulations
2. Inspection of the "record of navigational activities" log to establish when the installation has been switched off and if this has been reported to the Flag Administration (SOLAS 1974 regulation V/19-1.7.2 and resolution MSC.263(84), para 4.4.1); and
3. Ensuring that any conformance test report is issued on behalf of the Flag State, even by itself or by an authorised application service provider (see MSC.1/Circ.1377/Rev.11 and updated versions as shown in GISIS), available for a vessel that has an LRIT installation.

10.1.4 Deficiencies Warranting Detention

A Port State Control Officer should use professional judgement to determine whether to detain the vessel until any noted deficiencies are corrected or to permit a vessel to sail with deficiencies.[3] To assist the Port State Control Officer in their assessment, the following deficiencies should be considered of such nature that they may warrant the detention of a vessel:

1. Absence of a valid LRIT conformance test report; and
2. The vessel's master or the responsible officer is not familiar with essential shipboard operational procedures relating to LRIT.

Taking account of the guidance found in the *Guidance on the implementation of the LRIT system* (MSC.1/Circ.1298), Port State Control Officers are also advised that vessels should not be detained if the LRIT installation on board works but the shoreside installation or

---

[3] SOLAS 1974 regulation V/16.2 states: "while all reasonable steps shall be taken to maintain the equipment required by this chapter in efficient working order, malfunctions of that equipment shall not be considered as making the vessel unseaworthy or as a reason for delaying the vessel in ports where repair facilities are not readily available, provided suitable arrangements are made by the vessel's master to take the inoperative equipment or unavailable information into account in planning and executing a safe voyage to a port where repairs can take place".

organisation is not able to receive, relay or process the information. Port State Control Officers are advised that a Flag State may issue a short-term certificate; this could happen if, following a successful inspection for the issuance of a conformance test report, the ASP has not been able to issue a document yet, or if the ASP is not able to perform a conformance test in due time upon the request of the shipowner.

Port State Control Under Tonnage 1969

11

The International Convention on Tonnage Measurement of Ships, 1969 (TONNAGE 1969), which came into force on 18 July 1982, applies to:

1. New vessels, i.e., vessels the keels of which were laid on or after 18 July 1982; and
2. Existing vessels, i.e., vessels the keels of which were laid before 18 July 1982, as from 18 July 1994, except that for the purpose of application of SOLAS 1974, MARPOL and STCW 1978, the following interim schemes indicated in paragraph 2 may apply.

In accordance with the interim schemes adopted by the IMO[1] the Administration may, at the request of the shipowner, use the gross tonnage determined in accordance with national rules prior to the coming into force of TONNAGE 1969 for the following vessels:

1. For the purposes of SOLAS 1974:
   a. vessels the keels of which were laid before 1 January 1986
   b. in respect of SOLAS 1974 regulation IV/3, vessels the keels of which were laid on or after 1 January 1986 but before 18 July 1994; and
   c. cargo vessels of less than 1,600 tons gross tonnage (as determined under the national tonnage rules) the keels of which were laid on or after 1 January 1986 but before 18 July 1994; and
2. For the purposes of MARPOL, vessels of less than 400 tons gross tonnage (as determined under the national tonnage rules) the keels of which were laid before 18 July 1994.

---

[1] Resolutions A.494(XII) in respect of SOLAS 1974, A.540(13) in respect of STCW 78, and A.541(13) in respect of MARPOL.

© The Author(s), under exclusive license to Springer Nature Switzerland AG 2025
A. A. Olsen and F. Karkori, *Ship's Officer's Guide to Port State Control*,
Synthesis Lectures on Ocean Systems Engineering,
https://doi.org/10.1007/978-3-031-77502-4_11

For vessels to which the above interim schemes apply, a statement to the effect that the gross tonnage has been measured in accordance with the national tonnage rules should be included in the "REMARKS" column of the International Tonnage Certificate and in the footnote to the figure of the gross tonnage in the relevant SOLAS 1974 and MARPOL certificates. The Port State Control Officer should take the following actions as appropriate when deficiencies are found in relation to TONNAGE 1969:

1. If a vessel does not hold a valid International Tonnage Certificate, the vessel loses all privileges of TONNAGE 1969, and the Flag State should be informed without delay
2. If the required remarks and footnote are not included in the relevant certificates on vessels to which the interim schemes apply, this deficiency should be notified to the vessel's master; and
3. If the main characteristics of the vessel differ from those entered on the International Tonnage Certificate, so to lead to an increase in the gross tonnage or net tonnage, the Flag State should be informed without delay.

The control provisions of Article 12 of TONNAGE 1969 do not include the provision for detention of a vessel holding a valid International Tonnage Certificate.

Certification of Seafarers, Manning and Hours of Rest

12

The *International Convention for the Safety of Life at Sea* (SOLAS 1974) was adopted in 1974 and entered into force in 1980. Similarly, the *International Convention on Standards of Training, Certification and Watchkeeping for Seafarers* (STCW 1978) was adopted in 1978 and entered into force in 1984. Both have been amended several times since their entry into force. This chapter is intended to provide guidance for a harmonised approach to Port State Control inspections in compliance with SOLAS 1974 regulation V/14 (manning) and STCW 1978 regulation I/2 (seafarer certification) and chapter VIII (hours of rest). SOLAS 1974 regulation V/14.2 only applies to vessels covered by chapter I of SOLAS 1974. STCW 1978, as amended, applies to seafarers serving on board seagoing vessels. The STCW Code is divided into a mandatory part A and a non-mandatory part B. Part B of the STCW Code is not applicable during the Port State Control inspection. All passenger vessels regardless of size and all other vessels of 500 gross tonnage or more should have a minimum safe manning document or equivalent on board issued by the Flag State. Any new or single deficiency which is either a deficiency related to SOLAS 1974, STCW 1978 or other IMO conventions, should preferably be registered with these conventions' references.

12.1 Relevant Documentation

The documentation required for Port State Control inspection consists of:

1. Seafarer certification
2. Manning
3. Hours of rest.

12.1.1 Seafarer Certification

1. Certificate of competency
2. Certificate of proficiency
3. Endorsement attesting the recognition of a certificate (Flag State endorsement)
4. Documentary evidence (passenger vessels only); and
5. Medical certificate.

12.1.2 Manning

1. Minimum safe manning document; and
2. Muster list.

12.1.3 Hours of Rest

1. Table of vessel working arrangements and/or watch schedule; and
2. Records of daily hours of rest.

12.2 Definitions and Abbreviations

Certificate of Competency means a certificate issued and endorsed for masters, officers and Global Maritime Distress and Safety System (GMDSS) radio operators in accordance with the provisions of chapters II, III, IV or VII of STCW 1978 and entitling the lawful holder thereof to serve in the capacity and perform the functions involved at the level of responsibility specified therein.

Certificate of Proficiency means a certificate, other than a certificate of competency issued to a seafarer, stating that the relevant requirements of training, competencies or seagoing service in STCW 1978 have been met.

Documentary evidence means documentation, other than a Certificate of Competency or Certificate of Proficiency, used to establish that the relevant requirements of STCW 1978, as amended, have been met. The only documentary evidence required under STCW 1978, as amended, is issued to personnel meeting the mandatory minimum requirements for the training and qualifications of masters, officers, ratings and other personnel on passenger vessels (regulation V/2).

The following abbreviations have been used:

- CoC (Certificate of Competency)
- CoP (Certificate of Proficiency); and
- MSMD (minimum safe manning document).

12.3 Inspection of the Vessel

12.3.1 Pre-Boarding Preparation

Considering the type, size, engine power and other particulars of the vessel, the Port State Control Officer should be aware of the relevant requirements of SOLAS 1974 regulation V/14 and STCW 1978. The Port State Control Officer should be aware that resolutions are non-mandatory documents and not applicable during a Port State Control inspection. The Port State Control Officer should also identify if the Flag State is a Party to STCW 1978, as amended. If the Flag State is not a Party to the Convention or is a Party but not listed in MSC.1/Circ.1163, as amended, a more detailed inspection should be carried out.

12.3.2 Initial Inspection

12.3.2.1 Seafarer Certificates and Documents

The Port State Control Officer should examine the applicable documents listed above. The inspection should be limited to verification that seafarers serving on board, who are required to be certificated, hold the appropriate CoC, CoP and documentary evidence issued in accordance with chapters II, III, IV, V, VI and VII of STCW 1978, as amended, as well as their relevant Flag State endorsement, valid dispensation, or documentary proof that an application for an endorsement has been submitted to the Flag State Administration, where applicable. These documents are evidence of having successfully completed all required training and that the required standard of competence has been achieved. During the verification of the seafarers' certificates and documents, the Port State Control Officer should confirm that they are applicable to the vessel's characteristics, operation and their position on board. In accordance with the provision of Article VI, para 2 of

STCW 1978, certificates for vessel masters and officers should be endorsed by the issuing Administration in the form prescribed in regulation I/2 of the annex to the Convention. The certificates may be issued as one certificate with the required endorsement incorporated. If so incorporated, the form used should be that set forth in section A-I/2, para 1 of the STCW Code. The endorsement may also be issued as a separate document. If so, the form used should be that set out in section A-I/2, para 2 of the STCW Code. However, Administrations may use a format for certificates and endorsements different from those given in section A-I/2 of the STCW Code, provided that, at a minimum, the required information is provided in Roman characters and Arabic figures. Permitted variations to the format are set out in section A-I/2, para 4 of the STCW Code.

Certificates and endorsements issued as separate documents should each be assigned a unique number, except that endorsements attesting the issuance of a certificate may be assigned the same number as the certificate concerned, if number is unique. Certificates and endorsements issued as separate documents should include a date of expiry. The date of expiry on an endorsement issued as a separate document should not exceed five years from the date of issue and may never exceed the date of expiry on the certificate. A CoP issued to a master or an officer in accordance with regulation V/1-1 or V/1-2, as well as a CoC that has been issued by a State other than the Flag State of the vessel in which the seafarer is engaged, is required to be recognised by the vessel's Flag State. If the Port State Control Officer identifies that the Flag State has recognised a CoC or CoP from a Party not listed in MSC.1/Circ.1163, as amended, clarification should be sought from the Flag Administration. According to regulation I/10, para 4 of STCW 1978, certificates issued by or under the authority of a non-Party should not be recognised by the vessel's Flag State Administration. An Administration which recognises under regulation I/10 a CoC or CoP issued to vessel's master and officers should endorse that certificate to attest to its recognition. The form of the endorsement should be that found in section A-I/2, para 3 of the STCW Code. Incorrect wording or missing information may be a cause for suspicion regarding fraudulent certificates or endorsements.

Endorsements attesting to the recognition of a certificate should each be assigned a unique number; however, they may be assigned the same number as the certificate concerned, if number is unique. Endorsements attesting to the recognition of a certificate should include a date of expiry. The date of expiry on an endorsement attesting to the recognition may never exceed the date of expiry on the certificate being recognised. The capacity in which the holder of a certificate is authorised to serve should be identified in the form of endorsement in terms identical to those used in the applicable safe manning requirements of the Administration. This may result in slight variations of terminology between the original CoC and the endorsement to the recognition. Seafarers must have their original CoC on board as well as any original endorsements to the recognition. An endorsement attesting the recognition of a certificate should not entitle a seafarer to serve in a higher capacity than the original CoC. If circumstances require it, a Flag State Administration may permit a seafarer to serve for a period not exceeding three months on

12.3 Inspection of the Vessel

vessels entitled to fly its Flag while holding a valid CoC issued by another party and valid for service on that party's vessels. If such a situation exists, documentary proof must be readily available that an application for endorsement has been made to the Administration of the Flag State. This is often referred to as the confirmation of receipt of application (CRA). This provision allows Administrations to permit seafarers to serve on their vessels while the application for recognition is being processed. If an endorsement to attest recognition or certificate of competency has expired or has not been issued or documentary proof of application for endorsement is not readily available, the Port State Control Officer should consider whether the vessel can comply with STCW 1978 regulation I/4.1.2 regarding the numbers and certificates on board complying with the applicable safe manning requirements of the Flag State. This may be considered a deficiency in accordance with regulation I/4.2.4 and rectified before departure or detention may be applied. The Port State Control Officer carrying out the inspection should forthwith inform, in writing, the master of the vessel and the Consul or, in his absence, the nearest diplomatic representative or the maritime authority of the State whose Flag the vessel is entitled to fly, so that appropriate action may be taken.

In cases of suspected intoxication of vessel's masters, officers and/or other seafarers while performing designated safety, security and marine environmental protection duties, the appropriate authorities of the port and Flag State should be notified in accordance with Chaps. 3 and 4 of the *Procedures for Port State Control*. Seafarers should have a valid medical certificate and have completed applicable familiarisation on board the vessel. If such crew members are assigned to any designated safety, security or pollution prevention duties, they must be trained and qualified for such duties in accordance with the applicable chapter of the STCW Code. In accordance with section A-VI/1, para 5 of the STCW Code, the Flag State Administration may exempt the seafarers engaged on vessels other than passenger vessels of more than 500 gross tonnage on international voyages and tankers from some of the requirements of that section.

12.3.3 Manning

The Port State Control Officer should examine the applicable documents listed above. The guiding principles for Port State Control of the manning of a foreign vessel should be:

1. Verification that the numbers and certificates of the seafarers serving on board are in conformity with the applicable safe manning requirements of the Flag State; and
2. Verification that the vessel and its personnel conform to the international provisions as laid down in SOLAS 1974 and STCW 1978.

If a vessel is manned in accordance with an MSMD or equivalent document issued by the Flag State, the Port State Control Officer should accept that the vessel is safely manned unless the document has clearly been issued without regard to the principles contained in the relevant instruments, in which case the Port State Control Officer should consult the Flag State Administration. If the Flag State Administration has not issued a safe manning document or equivalent due to the vessel's size the Port State Control Officer should examine the CoC, CoP and their relevant Flag State endorsement for the crew and compare with the requirements of STCW 1978. Regarding the number of seafarers, the Port State Control Officer should then use their professional judgement, considering chapter VIII of STCW 1978 and the STCW Code and the duration and area of the next voyage, to determine if it can be undertaken safely. The Port State Control Officer should note the number of seafarers on board during the previous voyage as another indicator of standard manning levels for the vessel. The Port State Control Officer should consult the Flag State Administration if additional information is necessary. If an endorsement to attest recognition has expired or has not been issued or documentary proof of CRA is not readily available, the Port State Control Officer should consider whether the vessel can comply with the applicable safe manning requirements of the Flag State Administration. In cases where the Port State Control Officer finds that additional information is necessary, the Flag State Administration should be consulted.

If the Flag State does not respond to the request, this should be considered as clear grounds for a more detailed inspection to ensure that the number and composition of the crew are in accordance with the principles laid down above. The vessel should only be allowed to proceed to sea if it is safe to do so, considering the criteria for detention. In any such case, the minimum standards to be applied should be no more stringent than those applied to vessels flying the Flag of the Port State.

12.3.4 Hours of Rest

All persons who are assigned duty as officer in charge of a watch (OOW) or as a rating forming part of a watch (RFPW) and those whose duties involve designated safety, security and environmental protection duties shall be provided with a rest period of not less than:

1. A minimum of 10 h of rest in any 24-h period; and
2. 77 h in any seven-day period.

The hours of rest may be divided into no more than two periods, one of which shall be at least 6 h in length, and the intervals between consecutive periods of rest shall not exceed 14 h. The Port State Control Officer should examine the applicable documents, specifically the watch schedule and the records of daily hours of rest. The Port State Control Officer may inspect the seafarer's personal copy of their own records pertaining to the hours of rest being held by the seafarer on board to verify that the records are accurate. The watch schedule should be in a standardised format,[1] easily accessible to the crew and posted in the working language or languages of the vessel, and in English. Daily hours of rest shall be maintained in a standardised format, in the working language or languages of the vessel, and in English. The Port State Control Officer should consider that seafarers who are on call, such as when a machinery space is unattended, are to be provided with an adequate compensatory rest period if the normal period is disturbed by call-out to work. While assessing hours of rest, the Port State Control Officer should take account of any emergency conditions encountered which required a seafarer to perform additional hours of work for the immediate safety of the vessel. In such cases, the vessel's master should be consulted for an explanation of the events and how impacted seafarers were provided with an adequate period of rest. Flag State Administrations may provide exceptions to the requirements stated above for no more than two consecutive weeks provided that the rest period for the seafarer is not less than 70 h in any seven-day period.

12.3.5 Clear Grounds

Clear grounds are defined in section 1.7.2 of the *Procedures for Port State Control*. In addition to the general examples of clear grounds, the specific occurrences below, as outlined in para 1.3 of regulation I/4 of STCW 1978, are considered as factors leading to a more detailed inspection:

1. The vessel has been involved in a collision, grounding or stranding; or
2. There has been a discharge of substances from the vessel when under way, at anchor or at berth which is illegal under any international convention; or
3. The vessel has been manoeuvred in an erratic or unsafe manner whereby routeing measures adopted by IMO or safe navigation practices and procedures have not been followed; or
4. The vessel is otherwise being operated in such a manner as to pose a danger to persons, property or the environment, or a compromise to security.

---

[1] The *IMO/ILO Guidelines for the development of tables of seafarers' shipboard working arrangements and formats of records of seafarers' hours of work or hours of rest* may be used.

12.3.6 More Detailed Inspection

The Port State Control Officer should:

1. Verify that seafarers are sufficiently rested and otherwise fit for duty for the first watch at the commencement of the intended voyage and for subsequent relieving watches; this may be done by comparing records of daily hours of rest with the requirements in STCW 1978 for an appropriate period, which should at least include, whenever possible, the seven-day period immediately prior to departure; the rest period must reflect actual hours worked
2. Verify a sufficient number of certificates from all departments to demonstrate that the vessel and the composition of the crew complies with the MSMD and requirements of STCW 1978; and
3. Verify that navigational or engineering watch arrangements conform to the requirements specified for the vessel in the MSMD by the Flag State and the requirements of STCW 1978 regulation VIII/2 and STCW Code section A-VIII/2.

An assessment of seafarers can only be conducted by the Port State if there are clear grounds for believing that the ability of the seafarers of the vessel to maintain watchkeeping and security standards, as appropriate, as required by STCW 1978 is not being maintained because any of the situations stated in points 1, 2 and/or 3 above have occurred:

1. The assessment procedure provided in STCW 1978 regulation I/4, para 1.3, should take the form of a verification that members of the crew who are required to be competent do in fact possess the necessary skills related to the occurrence
2. It should be borne in mind when making this assessment that onboard procedures are relevant to the ISM Code and that the provisions of STCW 1978 are confined to the competence to safely execute those procedures
3. Control procedures under STCW 1978 should be confined to the standards of competence of the individual seafarers on board and their skills related to watchkeeping as defined in part A of the STCW Code. Onboard assessment of competency should commence with verification of the certificates of the seafarers
4. Notwithstanding verification of the certificate, the assessment under STCW 1978 regulation I/4, para 1.3 can require the seafarer to demonstrate the related competency at the place of duty. Such demonstration may include verification that operational requirements in respect of watchkeeping standards have been met and that there is a proper response to emergency situations within the seafarer's level of competence
5. In the assessment, only the methods for demonstrating competence together with the criteria for its evaluation and the scope of the standards given in part A of the STCW Code should be used. In cases where there is doubt about knowledge of operational use

of equipment, the relevant officer or crew member should be asked to perform a functional test. Failure to perform a functional test could indicate the lack of familiarisation or competency; and

6. Assessment of competency related to security should be conducted for those seafarers with specific security duties only in case of clear grounds, as provided for in chapter XI-2 of SOLAS 1974, by the competent security authority. In all other cases, it should be confined to the verification of the certificates and/or endorsements of the seafarers.

12.4 Follow-Up Action

12.4.1 Possible Action

Possible action to be considered by the Port State Control Officer for the control in compliance with SOLAS 1974 or STCW 1978 may be dealt with in the following ways:

1. Exercise of control with respect to the documentation concerning the vessel; and
2. Exercise of control with respect to the documentation for individual seafarers on board.

12.4.2 Possible Deficiencies

The following is a non-exhaustive list of possible deficiencies:

12.4.2.1 Seafarers' Documentation

1. No CoC, CoP, Flag State endorsements or proof that an application for an endorsement has been submitted (STCW 1978 regulations I/4.2.1 and I/10)
2. Special training requirements: mandatory basic or advanced training or endorsement not presented
3. No evidence of basic training, or other certificate of proficiency, if not included in a qualification certificate held (STCW 1978 regulations VI/1, VI/1.2, VI/3, VI/4 and VI/6); and
4. Information or evidence that the vessel's master or crew are not familiar with essential shipboard operations relating to the safety of vessels or the prevention of pollution, or that such operations have not been carried out.

12.4.2.2 Manning

5. No MSMD or the manning (number or qualification) not in accordance with the MSMD (SOLAS 1974 regulation V/14 and STCW 1978 regulation I/4.2.2); and
6. Unqualified person on duty (STCW 1978 regulation I/4.2.4).

12.4.2.3 Hours of Rest

7. Watch schedule not posted or not being followed (STCW 1978 regulations I/4.2.3 and I/4.2.5 and STCW Code A-VIII/1.5)
8. The absence of a table of shipboard working arrangements or of records of rest of seafarers (STCW Code A-VIII/1.7)
9. The records of hours of rest are inaccurate or incomplete (STCW Code A-VIII/1.7); and
10. The watchkeeper is receiving less than 10 h rest in any 24-h period (i.e., working in excess of 14 h) or 77 h rest in any seven-day period (STCW Code A-VIII/1).

12.4.3 Deficiencies That May Warrant Detention

Deficiencies which may be deemed to pose a danger to persons, property or the environment, as specified in para 2 of regulation I/4 of STCW 1978, as amended:

1. Failure of seafarers to hold a certificate, to have an appropriate certificate, to have a valid dispensation or to provide documentary proof that an application for an endorsement has been submitted to the Administration in accordance with regulation I/10, para 5
2. Failure to comply with the applicable safe manning requirement of the Administration
3. Failure of navigational or engineering watch arrangements to conform to the requirements specified for the vessel by the Administration
4. Absence in a watch of a person qualified to operate equipment essential to safe navigation, safety radiocommunications or the prevention of marine pollution; and
5. Inability to provide, for the first watch at the commencement of a voyage and for subsequent relieving watches, persons who are sufficiently rested and otherwise fit for duty.

Failure to correct any of the deficiencies, insofar as it has been determined by the Port State Control Officer that they pose a danger to persons, property or the environment, shall be the only grounds under STCW 1978, as amended, on which a vessel may be detained. Examples of detainable deficiencies according to SOLAS 1974 and STCW 1978 are listed below.

12.4.3.1 Vessel-Related Deficiencies

1. MSMD or equivalent not presented (SOLAS 1974 regulation V/14.2); and
2. Records of daily hours of rest are not on board (STCW Code A-VIII/1.7).

12.4.3.2 Seafarers' Documentation

3. Not available or serious discrepancy in the CoC (STCW 1978 regulation I/4.2.1)
4. Absence in watch of a radio operator (general/restricted GMDSS); certificates and endorsement not available (STCW 1978 regulations I/4.2.1, I/4.2.2, I/4.2.3, I/4.2.4 and II/1.2.1)
5. Documentation for personnel with designated safety, security and marine environmental duties not available (STCW 1978 regulations I/4.2.1, I/4.2.2, I/4.2.3 and I/4.2.4)
6. Expired certificates (STCW 1978 regulation I/4.2.1), and for medical certificates also refer to STCW 1978 regulations I/9.6 and I/9.7; and
7. Evidence that a certificate has been fraudulently obtained or the holder of a certificate is not the person to whom that certificate was originally issued.

12.4.4 Actions to Be Considered

12.4.4.1 Vessel Related Deficiencies

If the actual number of crew or composition does not conform to the manning document, the port State should request the Flag State for advice as to whether the vessel should be allowed to sail with the actual number of crew and composition of crew. Such a request and response should be by the most expedient means and either party may request the communication in writing. If the actual crew number or composition is not brought into compliance with the MSMD or the Flag State does not advise that the vessel may sail, the vessel may be considered for detention after the criteria set out above have been accounted for.

Before detaining the vessel, the Port State Control Officer should consider the following:

1. Length and nature of the intended voyage or service
2. Whether or not the deficiency poses a danger to vessel, persons on board or the environment
3. Whether or not appropriate rest periods of the crew can be observed
4. Size and type of vessel and equipment provided; and the
5. Nature of cargo.

12.4.4.2 Deficiency-Related

When the manning is not in accordance with the MSMD and no Flag State endorsements or no "documentary proof of application" can be presented, the Port State should consult the Flag State whenever possible, accounting for time differences or other conditions. However, if it is not possible to establish contact with the Flag State, the Port State should forthwith inform, in writing, the master of the vessel and the Consul or, in their absence, the nearest diplomatic representative or the maritime authority of the State whose Flag the vessel is entitled to fly, so that appropriate action may be taken. In cases where an unqualified seafarer has been on duty and/or the watch schedule has not been followed, the Flag State should be informed, and this could be considered as an ISM deficiency. In cases where there is a seafarer on duty who is not qualified to carry out an operation, that specific operation should be stopped immediately.

12.5 Note on Reporting Deficiencies

The Port State Control Officer should be aware that, in addition to SOLAS 1974 and STCW 1978, there may be other applicable international instruments. The Port State Control Officer should decide which one is the most appropriate.

13. Port State Control Inspections Under MARPOL Annex VI

This chapter is intended to provide basic guidance on the conduct of Port State Control inspections for compliance with MARPOL Annex VI (hereinafter referred to as "the Annex") and afford consistency in the conduct of these inspections, the recognition of deficiencies and the application of control procedures.

13.1 Inspections of Vessels Required to Carry the IAPP Certificate and/or the IEE Certificate

13.1.1 Initial Inspections

The Port State Control Officer should ascertain the status of the vessel as regards application of regulations 20 and 21 of the Annex, the vessel's tonnage, the date of vessel construction and the date of installation of equipment on board which are subject to the provisions of the Annex, to confirm which regulations of the Annex are applicable. On boarding and introduction to the vessel's master or responsible vessel's officer, the Port State Control Officer should examine the following documents, where applicable:

1. The International Air Pollution Prevention Certificate (IAPP Certificate) (regulation VI/6), including its Supplement
2. The International Energy Efficiency Certificate (IEE Certificate) (regulation VI/6) including its Supplement

3. The Engine International Air Pollution Prevention Certificate (EIAPP Certificate) (para 2.2 of the NO_X Technical Code) including its Supplement, for each applicable marine diesel engine
4. The Technical File (para 2.3.4 of the NO_X Technical Code) for each applicable marine diesel engine
5. Depending on the method used for demonstrating NO_X compliance for each applicable marine diesel engine:
   a. the Record Book of Engine Parameters for each marine diesel engine (para 6.2.2.7 of the NO_X Technical Code) demonstrating compliance with regulation VI/13 by means of the marine diesel engine parameter check method; or
   b. documentation relating to the simplified measurement method; or
   c. documentation related to the direct measurement and monitoring method.
6. For a vessel to which regulation VI/13.5.1 applies for a particular NO_X Tier III emission control area and that has one or more installed marine diesel engines certified to both Tier II and Tier III or which has one or more marine diesel engines certified to Tier II only,[1] the required logbook and the recordings for the tier and on/off status of those marine diesel engines while the vessel is within an applicable NO_X Tier III emission control area
7. The Approved Method File (regulation VI/13.7)
8. The written procedures covering fuel oil changeover operations (in a working language or languages understood by the crew) where separate fuel oils are used to achieve compliance (regulation VI/14.6)
9. The approved documentation relating to exceptions and/or exemptions granted under regulation VI/3
10. The approved documentation (SECC where issued, ETM, OMM, SECP) and relating to any installed exhaust gas cleaning system (EGCS) or equivalent means, to reduce SO_X emissions (regulation VI/4)
11. EGCS monitoring records, checking they have been retained and show compliance. Additionally, checking that the EGCS Record Book including nitrate discharge data and performance records,[2] or approved alternative, has been duly maintained
12. The BDN and representative samples or records thereof (regulation VI/18)
13. The copy of the type approval certificate of applicable shipboard incinerator (resolutions MEPC.76(40) or MEPC.244(66))
14. The Ozone-depleting Substances Record Book (regulation VI/12.6)

---

[1] Unified interpretation of regulation 13.5.3 set out in MEPC.1/Circ.795/Rev.5.

[2] In assessing the emission ratio and discharge water records the Port State Control Officer should be mindful that such factors as transient engine operation or analyser performance outputs may result in isolated "spikes" in the recorded output which, while these measurements in themselves may be above the required emission ratio or discharge water limit values, do not indicate that overall the EGCS was not being operated and controlled as required and hence should not be taken as evidence of non-compliance with the requirements.

15. The VOC Management Plan (regulation VI/15.6)
16. Any notification to the vessel's Flag Administration issued by the vessel's master or officer in charge of the bunker operation together with any available commercial documentation relevant to non-compliant bunker delivery, regulation VI/18.2
17. If the vessel has not been able to obtain compliant fuel oil, the notification to the vessel's Flag Administration and the competent authority of the relevant port of destination
18. The Ship Energy Efficiency Management Plan (SEEMP) including, where applicable, the methodology that will be used to collect the data required by regulation 22A of the Annex and the associated Confirmation of Compliance in respect of that methodology; and
19. For the year 2019 and onwards that the vessel has, no later than 1 June of each following year, the Statement of Compliance—Fuel Oil Consumption Reporting.

The record books referenced in sub-paras 1, 5, 10 and 13 above may be presented in an electronic format. A declaration from the Administration should be viewed to accept this electronic record book. If a declaration cannot be provided, a hard copy record book will need to be presented for examination. As a preliminary check, the IAPP Certificate's validity should be confirmed by verifying that the Certificate is properly completed and signed and that required surveys have been performed. Through examining the Supplement to the IAPP Certificate, the Port State Control Officer may establish how the vessel is equipped for the prevention of air pollution. In the case where the BDN or the representative sample as required by regulation VI/18 presented to the vessel are not in compliance with the relevant requirements (the BDN is set out in appendix V of MARPOL Annex VI), the vessel's master or officer in charge of the bunker operation may have documented that through a notification to the vessel's Flag Administration with copies to the port authority under whose jurisdiction the vessel did not receive the required documentation pursuant to the bunkering operation and to the bunker deliverer. In addition, if the BDN shows compliant fuel, but the vessel's master has independent test results of the fuel oil sample taken by the vessel during the bunkering which indicates non-compliance, the vessel's master may have documented that through a notification to the vessel's Flag Administration with copies to the competent authority of the relevant port of destination, the Administration under whose jurisdiction the bunker deliverer is located and to the bunker deliverer. In all cases, a copy may be retained on board the vessel, together with any available commercial documentation, for the subsequent scrutiny of Port State Control. As a preliminary check, the IEE Certificate's validity should be confirmed by verifying that the Certificate is properly completed and signed.

13.1.2 Initial Inspection on Vessels Equipped with Equivalent Means of SO$_x$ Compliance

On vessels equipped with equivalent means of compliance, the Port State Control Officer will look at:

1. Evidence that the vessel has received an appropriate approval for any installed equivalent means (approved, under trial or being commissioned)
2. Evidence that the vessel is using an equivalent means, as identified on the Supplement of the IAPP certificate, for fuel oil combustion units on board or that compliant fuel oil is used in equipment not so covered; and
3. BDNs on board[3] which indicate that the fuel oil is intended to be used in combination with an equivalent means of SO$_x$ compliance or the vessel is subject to a relevant exemption to conduct trials for SO$_x$ emission reduction and control technology research.

In the case where an EGCS is not in compliance with the relevant requirements for other than transitory periods and isolated spikes in the recorded output, the vessel's master or officer in charge may have documented that through a notification to the vessel's Flag Administration with copies to the competent authority of the relevant port of destination, and present those corrective actions taken in order to rectify the situation in accordance with the guidance given in the EGCS Technical Manual. If a malfunction occurs in the instrumentation for the monitoring of emission to air or the monitoring of wash water discharge to sea, the vessel may have alternative documentation demonstrating compliance.[4]

13.1.3 Initial Inspection Within an Emission Control Area

When a vessel is inspected in a port in an emission control area (ECA) designated for SO$_x$ emission control, the Port State Control Officer should look at:

1. Evidence of fuel oil delivered to and used on board with a sulphur content of not more than 0.10% m/m through the BDNs and appropriate onboard records including records

---

[3] Resolution MEPC.305(73) on *Prohibition on the carriage of non-compliant fuel oil for combustion purposes for propulsion or operation on board a vessel* is not applicable to fuel oil carried as cargo or for vessels fitted with an approved equivalent means of compliance.

[4] MEPC.1/Circ.883 on *Guidance on indication of ongoing compliance in the case of the failure of a single monitoring instrument, and recommended actions to take if the exhaust gas cleaning system (EGCS) fails to meet the provisions of the 2015 EGCS Guidelines (resolution MEPC.259(68)):* vessels should have documented notification of system non-compliance to relevant authorities.

of bunkering operations as set out in the Oil Record Book Part 1 (regulations VI/18.5 and VI/14.4); and

2. For those vessels using separate fuel oils for compliance with regulation VI/14, evidence of a written procedure (in a working language or languages understood by the crew) and records of changeover to fuel oil with a sulphur content of not more than 0.10% m/m before entering the ECA such that compliant fuel was being used while sailing in the entire ECA as required in regulation VI/14.6.

When a vessel to which regulation VI/13.5.1 applies for a particular NO_x Tier III emission control area is inspected in a port in that area, the Port State Control Officer should look at:

1. The records in respect of the tier and on/off status, together with any changes to that status while within that NO_x Tier III emission control area, which are to be logged as required by regulation VI/13.5.3 in respect of an installed marine diesel engine certified to both Tier II and Tier III or which is certified to Tier II only[5]; and
2. The status of an installed marine diesel engine which is certified to both Tier II and Tier III showing that that engine was operating in its Tier III condition on entry into that NO_x Tier III emission control area and that status was always maintained while that marine diesel engine was in operation within that area; or
3. The records related to the conditions associated with an exemption granted under regulation VI/13.5.4, checking they have been logged as required by that exemption and that the terms and duration of that exemption have been complied with as required.

13.1.4 Initial Inspection Outside an ECA or First Port After Transiting an ECA

When a vessel is inspected in a port outside the ECA the Port State Control Officer will look to the same documentation and evidence as during inspections in ports inside the ECA. The Port State Control Officer should, specifically, look at:

1. Evidence that the sulphur content of the fuel oil is in accordance with regulation VI/14.1[6] through the BDNs and appropriate onboard records including records of bunkering operations as set out in the Oil Record Book Part 1 (regulations VI/18.5 and VI/14.4); and

---

[5] Unified interpretation of regulation 13.5.3 set out in MEPC.1/Circ.795/Rev.5.
[6] Resolution MEPC.305(73) on *Prohibition on the carriage of non-compliant fuel oil for combustion purposes for propulsion or operation on board a vessel* is not applicable to fuel oil carried as cargo or for vessels fitted with an approved equivalent means of compliance.

2. Evidence of a written procedure (in a working language or languages understood by the crew) and records of changeover from fuel oil with a sulphur content of not more than 0.10% m/m after leaving the ECA such that compliant fuel was being used while sailing in the entire ECA.

When a vessel to which regulation VI/13.5.1 applies for a particular NO_x Tier III emission control area is inspected in a port outside that area, the Port State Control Officer should look at the vessel's records to ensure that the relevant requirements were complied with for the whole period the vessel was operating in that area.

13.2 Outcome of Initial Inspection

If the certificates and documents are valid and appropriate and, after an inspection of the vessel to check that the overall condition of the vessel meets generally accepted international rules and standards, the Port State Control Officer's general impressions and observations on board confirm a good standard of maintenance, the inspection should be considered satisfactorily concluded. If, however, the Port State Control Officer's general impressions or observations on board give clear grounds for believing that the condition of the vessel or its equipment does not correspond substantially with the particulars of the certificates or the documents, the Port State Control Officer should proceed to a more detailed inspection. "Clear grounds" to conduct a more detailed inspection include:

1. Evidence that certificates required by the Annex are missing or clearly invalid
2. Evidence that documents required by the Annex are missing or clearly invalid
3. The absence or malfunctioning of equipment or arrangements specified in the certificates or documents
4. The presence of equipment or arrangements not specified in the certificates or documents
5. Evidence from the Port State Control Officer's general impressions or observations that serious deficiencies exist in the equipment or arrangements specified in the certificates or documents
6. Information or evidence that the vessel's master or crew are not familiar with essential shipboard operations relating to the prevention of air pollution, or that such operations have not been carried out
7. Evidence of inconsistency between information in the BDN and para 2.3 of the Supplement to the IAPP certificate
8. Evidence that an equivalent means has not been used as required; or
9. Evidence, for example by fuel calculators, that the quantity of bunkered compliant fuel oil is inconsistent with the vessel's voyage plan; and

10. Receipt of a report or complaint containing information that the vessel appears to be non-compliant including but not limited to information from remote sensing surveillance of SO_x emissions or portable fuel oil sulphur content measurement devices indicating that a vessel appears to use non-compliant fuel while in operation/under way
11. Evidence that the tier and/or on/off status of applicable installed marine diesel engines has not been maintained correctly or as required
12. Receipt of a report or complaint containing information that one or more of the installed marine diesel engines has not been operated in accordance with the provisions of the respective Technical File or the requirements relevant to a particular NO_x Tier III emission control area; and
13. Receipt of a report or complaint containing information that the conditions attached to an exemption granted under regulation VI/13.5.4 have not been complied with.

13.3 More Detailed Inspections

The Port State Control Officer should verify that:

1. There are effectively implemented maintenance procedures for the equipment containing ozone-depleting substances; and
2. There are no deliberate emissions of ozone-depleting substances.

To verify that each installed marine diesel engine with a power output of more than 130 kW is approved by the Administration in accordance with the NO_x Technical Code and maintained appropriately, the Port State Control Officer should pay particular attention to the following:

1. Examine such marine diesel engines to be consistent with the EIAPP Certificate and its Supplement, Technical File and, if applicable, Record Book of Engine Parameters or Onboard Monitoring Manual and related data
2. Examine marine diesel engines specified in the Technical Files to verify that no unapproved modifications, which may affect NO_x emission, have been made to the marine diesel engines
3. In the case of an installed marine diesel engine certified to Tier III, check that the required records, if applicable, in accordance with regulation VI/13.5.1 or in the Technical File, including those required by 2.3.6 of the NO_x Technical Code, have been maintained as necessary and that the marine diesel engine, including any NO_x control device and associated ancillary systems and equipment, including, where fitted, bypass arrangements, is maintained in accordance with the associated Technical File and is in good order

4. If applicable, examine whether the conditions attached to an exemption granted under regulation VI/13.5.4 have been complied with as required
5. Examine marine diesel engines with a power output of more than 5,000 kW and a per cylinder displacement at or above 90 L installed on a vessel constructed on or after 1 January 1990 but prior to 1 January 2000 to verify that they are certified, if so required, in accordance with regulation VI/13.7
6. In the case of vessels constructed before 1 January 2000, verify that any marine diesel engine which has been subject to a major conversion, as defined in regulation VI/13, has been approved by the Administration; and
7. Emergency marine diesel engines intended to be used solely in case of emergency are still in use for this purpose.

The Port State Control Officer should check and verify whether fuel oil complies with the provisions of regulation VI/14 accounting for appendix VI[7] of MARPOL Annex VI. The Port State Control Officer should pay attention to the record required in regulation VI/14.6 to identify the sulphur content of fuel oil used by the vessel depending on the area of trade, or that other equivalent approved means have been applied as required, the fuel oil consumed in and outside the ECA, and that there is enough fuel in compliance with regulation VI/14 to reach the next port destination. Where EGCS is used, the Port State Control Officer should check that it has been installed and operated, together with its monitoring systems, in accordance with the associated approved documentation according to the survey procedures as established in the OMM. If the vessel is equipped with an EGCS as an equivalent means of SO_x compliance, the Port State Control Officer should verify that the system is properly functioning, is in operation, there are continuous-monitoring systems with tamper-proof data recording and processing devices,[8] if applicable, and the records demonstrate the necessary compliance when set against the limits given in the approved documentation and applies to relevant fuel combustion units on board. Checking can include but is not limited to emissions ratio, pH, PAH, turbidity readings as limit values given in ETM-A or ETM-B and operation parameters as listed in the system documentation.

If the vessel is a tanker, as defined in regulation VI/2.21, the Port State Control Officer should verify that the vapour collection system approved by the Administration, accounting for MSC/Circ.585, is installed, if required under regulation VI/15. If the vessel is a tanker carrying crude oil, the Port State Control Officer should verify that there is on board an approved VOC Management Plan. The Port State Control Officer should verify that prohibited materials are not incinerated. The Port State Control Officer should verify that shipboard incineration of sewage sludge or sludge oil in boilers or marine power

---

[7] Amendments to MARPOL VI, appendix VI, Verification procedures for a MARPOL Annex VI fuel oil sample.

[8] Equivalent emission values for emission abatement methods are 4.3 and 21.7 SO_2 (ppm)/CO_2 (% v/v) for marine fuels with a sulphur content of 0.10 and 0.50 (% m/m) respectively.

13.3 More Detailed Inspections

plants is not undertaken while the vessel is inside ports, harbours or estuaries (regulation VI/16.4). The Port State Control Officer should verify that the shipboard incinerator, if required by regulation VI/16.6.1, is approved by the Administration. For these units, it should be verified that the incinerator is properly maintained, therefore the Port State Control Officer should examine whether:

1. The shipboard incinerator is consistent with the certificate of shipboard incinerator
2. The operational manual, to operate the shipboard incinerator within the limits provided in appendix IV to the Annex, is provided; and
3. The combustion chamber flue gas outlet temperature is always monitored the unit is in operation (regulation VI/16.9).

The Port State Control Officer should verify whether the vessel has been subject to a major conversion (regulation VI/2.24) or there have been changes to the vessel in respect of aspects which are covered by the EEDI Technical File. If there are clear grounds, the Port State Control Officer may examine operational or reporting procedures by confirming that:

1. The vessel's master or crew are familiar with the procedures to prevent emissions of ozone-depleting substances
2. The vessel's master or crew are familiar with the proper operation and maintenance of marine diesel engines, in accordance with their Technical Files or Approved Method file, as applicable, and with due regard for emission control areas for NO_x control
3. The vessel's master or crew are familiar with fuel oil bunkering procedures in connection to the respective BDN and onboard records including the Oil Record Book Part 1 (regulations VI/18.5 and VI/14.4) and retained samples as required by regulation VI/18
4. The vessel's master or crew are familiar with the correct operation of an EGCS or other equivalent means on board together with any applicable monitoring and recording, and record-keeping requirements
5. The vessel's master or crew are familiar and have undertaken the necessary fuel oil changeover procedures, or equivalent, associated with demonstrating compliance within an emission control area
6. The vessel's master or crew are familiar with the garbage screening procedure to ensure that prohibited garbage is not incinerated
7. The vessel's master or crew are familiar with the operation of the shipboard incinerator, as required by regulation VI/16.6, within the limits provided in appendix IV to the Annex, in accordance with its operational manual
8. The vessel's master or crew are familiar with the regulation of emissions of VOCs, when the vessel is in ports or terminals under the jurisdiction of a Party to the 1997 Protocol to MARPOL 73/78 in which VOCs emissions are to be regulated, and are

familiar with the proper operation of a vapour collection system approved by the Administration (in case the vessel is a tanker as defined in regulation VI/2.21); and
9. The vessel's master or crew are familiar with the application of the VOC Management Plan, if applicable.

13.4 Detainable Deficiencies

In exercising their functions, the Port State Control Officer should use professional judgement to determine whether to detain the vessel until any noted deficiencies are corrected or to allow it to sail with certain deficiencies which do not pose an unreasonable threat of harm under the scope of the Annex provided, they will be addressed in a timely manner. In doing this, the Port State Control Officer should be guided by the principle that the requirements contained in the Annex, with respect to the construction, equipment and operation of the vessel, are essential for the protection of the marine environment, navigational safety or human health and that departure from these requirements could constitute an unreasonable threat of harm to the protection aspects mentioned and should be avoided. To assist the Port State Control Officer in their inspection, there follows a list of deficiencies which are considered, accounting for the provisions of regulation VI/3, to be of such a serious nature that they may warrant the detention of the vessel involved:

1. Absence of valid IAPP Certificate, EIAPP Certificates or Technical Files, if applicable
2. Absence of valid IEE Certificate, EEDI Technical File or SEEMP
3. Absence of a valid Statement of Compliance—Fuel Oil Consumption Reporting covering the year 2019 and onwards from 1 June of each following year
4. A marine diesel engine, with a power output of more than 130 kW, which is installed on board a vessel constructed on or after 1 January 2000, or a marine diesel engine having undergone a major conversion on or after 1 January 2000 which does not conform to its Technical File or where the required records have not been maintained as necessary or where it has not met the applicable requirements of the particular NO_x Tier III emission control area in which it is operating
5. A marine diesel engine, with a power output of more than 5,000 kW and a per cylinder displacement at or above 90 L, which is installed on board a vessel constructed on or after 1 January 1990 but prior to 1 January 2000, and an approved method for that engine has been certified by an Administration and was commercially available, for which an approved method is not installed after the first renewal survey specified in regulation VI/13.7.2

6. On vessels not equipped with equivalent means of SO_x compliance, based on the methodology of sample analysis in accordance with appendix VI[9] of MARPOL Annex VI, the sulphur content of any fuel oil being used or carried for use on board exceeds the applicable limit required by regulation VI/14. If the vessel's master claims that it was not possible to bunker compliant fuel oil, the Port State Control Officer should account for the provisions of regulation VI/18.2
7. On vessels equipped with equivalent means of SO_x compliance, absence of an appropriate approval for the equivalent means, which applies to relevant fuel combustion units on board. With respect to combustion units not connected to an EGCS, the sulphur content of any fuel oil being used on these combustion units exceeds the limits stipulated in regulation VI/14, taking accounting for the provisions of regulation VI/18.2
8. Non-compliance with the relevant requirements while operating within an ECA for SO_x and particulate matter control
9. An incinerator installed on board the vessel on or after 1 January 2000 does not comply with requirements contained in appendix IV to the Annex, or the standard specifications for shipboard incinerators developed by the IMO (resolutions MEPC.76(40) and MEPC.244(66)); and
10. The vessel's master or crew are not familiar with essential procedures regarding the operation of air pollution prevention equipment or reporting requirements as defined above.

13.5 Inspections of Vessels of Non-parties to the Annex and Other Vessels not Required to Carry the IAPP Certificate or the IEE Certificate

13.5.1 Vessels of Non-parties and Vessels not Required to Carry the IAPP Certificate

As this category of vessel is not provided with the IAPP Certificate, the Port State Control Officer should judge whether the condition of the vessel and its equipment satisfies the requirements set out in Chap. 3 of the Annex. In this respect, the Port State Control Officer should account for that, in accordance with Article 5(4) of MARPOL, no more favourable treatment is to be given to vessels of non-Parties. In all other respects the Port State Control Officer should be guided by the procedures for vessels referred to in the first section of this chapter and should be satisfied that the vessel and crew do not present a danger to those on board or an unreasonable threat of harm to the marine environment.

---

[9] Amendments to MARPOL VI, appendix VI, Verification procedures for a MARPOL Annex VI fuel oil sample.

If the vessel has a form of certification other than the IAPP Certificate, the Port State Control Officer may take such documentation into account in the evaluation of the vessel.

13.5.2 Vessels of Non-parties and Vessels not Required to Carry the IEE Certificate

As vessels of non-Parties are not provided with the IEE Certificate, the Port State Control Officer may examine equivalent documentation issued by that non-Party showing that the vessel is of a design no less energy-efficient than that required by chapter IV of the Annex. In addition, the vessel should have on board an energy efficiency management plan equivalent to that required for the SEEMP. Such vessels are not required to have documentation and procedures covering fuel oil consumption reporting and hence will not have a Statement of Compliance—Fuel Oil Consumption Reporting. Vessels of Parties which are not required to carry the IEE Certificate are not required to have a SEEMP or to have documentation and procedures covering fuel oil consumption reporting and hence will not have a Statement of Compliance—Fuel Oil Consumption Reporting.

13.5.3 Claims of Non-availability of Compliant Fuel Oil

In case non-availability of compliant fuel oil is claimed the vessel's master/owner must present a record of actions taken to attempt to bunker compliant fuel oil and provide evidence:

1. Of attempts to purchase compliant fuel oil in accordance with its voyage plan
2. If the fuel oil was not made available where expected, that attempts were made to locate alternative sources for such fuel oil; and
3. That despite best efforts to obtain compliant fuel oil no such fuel oil was made available for purchase.

Best efforts to procure compliant fuel oil include, but are not limited to, investigating alternative sources of fuel oil prior to commencing the voyage or en route. The vessel should not be required to deviate from its intended voyage or to unduly delay the voyage to achieve compliance. If the vessel provides the information, as above, the port State should account for all relevant circumstances and the evidence presented to determine the appropriate action to take, including not taking control measures. The vessel's master/owner may provide evidence as below to support their claim (not exhaustive):

1. A copy (or description) of the vessel's voyage plan, including the vessel's port of origin and port of destination

2. The time the vessel first received notice it would be conducting a voyage involving transit/arrival in the port and the vessel's location when it first received such notice
3. A description of the actions taken to attempt to achieve compliance, including a description of all attempts that were made to locate alternative sources of compliant fuel oil, and a description of the reason why compliant fuel was not available (for example, compliant fuel oil was not available at ports on the "intended voyage", fuel oil supply disruptions at port)
4. The cost of compliant fuel is not considered to be a valid basis for claiming non-availability of fuel
5. Names and addresses of the fuel oil suppliers contacted and the dates on which contact was made
6. In cases of fuel oil supply disruption, the name of the port at which the vessel was scheduled to receive compliant fuel oil and the name of the fuel supplier that is reporting the non-availability of compliant fuel oil
7. The availability of compliant fuel oil at the next port of call and plans to obtain that fuel oil; and
8. If applicable, identification and description of any operational constraints that prevented use of compliant fuel oil, for example, with respect to viscosity or other fuel oil parameters.

If, despite best efforts, it was not possible to procure compliant fuel oil the vessel's master/owner must notify the Port State Control authorities in the port of arrival and the Flag Administration (regulation VI/18.2.4).

Annex A

List of Certificates or Documentary Evidence Required Under STCW 1978

Refer to table B-I/2 of the STCW Code, as amended.

Part A
List of certificates and documents which to the extent applicable should be checked as a minimum during the inspection (as appropriate):

1. International Tonnage Certificate (TONNAGE 1969 Article 7)
2. Reports of previous port State control inspections
3. Passenger Ship Safety Certificate (SOLAS 1974 regulation I/12)
4. Cargo Ship Safety Construction Certificate (SOLAS 1974 regulation I/12)
5. Cargo Ship Safety Equipment Certificate (SOLAS 1974 regulation I/12)
6. Cargo Ship Safety Radio Certificate (SOLAS 1974 regulation I/12)
7. Cargo Ship Safety Certificate (SOLAS 1974 regulation I/12)
8. Exemption Certificate (SOLAS 1974 regulation I/12)
9. Minimum Safe Manning document (SOLAS 1974 regulation V/14.2)
10. International Load Line Certificate (1966) (LL 1966/LL PROT 1988 Article 16.1)
11. International Load Line Exemption Certificate (LL 1966/LL PROT 1988 Article 16.2)
12. International Oil Pollution Prevention Certificate (MARPOL Annex I regulation 7.1)
13. International Pollution Prevention Certificate for the Carriage of Noxious Liquid Substances in Bulk (NLS) (MARPOL Annex II regulation 9.1)
14. International Sewage Pollution Prevention Certificate (MARPOL Annex IV regulation 5.1 and MEPC.1/Circ.408)
15. International Air Pollution Prevention Certificate (MARPOL Annex VI regulation 6.1)
16. International Energy Efficiency Certificate (MARPOL Annex VI regulation 6)

17. International Ballast Water Management Certificate (BWM 2004 Article 9.1(a) and regulation E-2)
18. International Anti-Fouling System Certificate (AFS 2001 annex 4 regulation 2)
19. Declaration on AFS (AFS 2001 annex 4 regulation 5)
20. International Ship Security Certificate or Interim International Ship Security Certificate (ISPS Code part A/19 and appendices)
21. Certificates for masters, officers or ratings (STCW 1978 Article VI and regulation I/2, and STCW Code section A-I/2)
22. Copy of the Document of Compliance or a copy of the Interim Document of Compliance (SOLAS 1974 regulation IX/4.2 and ISM Code paras 13 and 14)
23. Safety Management Certificate or an Interim Safety Management Certificate (SOLAS 1974 regulation IX/4.3 and ISM Code paras 13 and 14)
24. International Certificate of Fitness for the Carriage of Liquefied Gases in Bulk, or the Certificate of Fitness for the Carriage of Liquefied Gases in Bulk, whichever is appropriate (IGC Code section 1.4 or GC Code section 1.6)
25. International Certificate of Fitness for the Carriage of Dangerous Chemicals in Bulk, or the Certificate of Fitness for the Carriage of Dangerous Chemicals in Bulk, whichever is appropriate (IBC Code section 1.5 or BCH Code section 1.6)
26. International Certificate of Fitness for the Carriage of INF Cargo (SOLAS 1974 regulation VII/16 and INF Code section 1.3)
27. Certificate of insurance or other financial security in respect of civil liability for oil pollution damage (CLC 69/92 Article VII.2)
28. Certificate of insurance or other financial security in respect of civil liability for bunker oil pollution damage (BUNKERS 2001 Article 7.2)
29. Certificate of insurance or other financial security in respect of liability for the removal of wrecks (Nairobi WRC 2007 Article 12)
30. High-Speed Craft Safety Certificate and Permit to Operate High-Speed Craft (SOLAS 1974 regulation X/3.2 and 1994/2000 HSC Code para 1.8.1 and section 1.9)
31. Document of Compliance with the special requirements for ships carrying dangerous goods (SOLAS 1974 regulation II-2/19.4)
32. Document of authorisation for the carriage of grain and grain loading manual (SOLAS 1974 regulation VI/9 and Grain Code section 3)
33. Condition Assessment Scheme (CAS) Statement of Compliance, CAS Final Report and Review Record (MARPOL Annex I regulations 20 and 21; resolution MEPC.94(46), as amended by resolutions MEPC.99(48), MEPC.112(50), MEPC.131(53), MEPC.155(55) and MEPC.236(65))
34. Continuous Synopsis Record (SOLAS 1974 regulation XI-1/5)
35. Oil Record Book, parts I and II (MARPOL Annex I regulations 17 and 36)
36. Cargo Record Book (MARPOL Annex II regulation 15)
37. Garbage Record Book (MARPOL Annex V regulation 10)

38. Garbage Management Plan (MARPOL Annex V regulation 10 and resolution MEPC.220(63))
39. Logbook and the recordings of the tier and on/off status of marine diesel engines (MARPOL Annex VI regulation 13.5.3)
40. Logbook for fuel oil changeover (MARPOL Annex VI regulation 14.6)
41. Ozone-depleting Substances Record Book (MARPOL Annex VI regulation 12.6)
42. Ballast Water Record Book (BWM 2004 Article 9.1(b) and regulation B-2)
43. Fixed gas fire extinguishing systems—Cargo Spaces Exemption Certificate and any list of cargoes (SOLAS 1974 regulation II-2/10.7.1.4)
44. Dangerous Goods Manifest Or Stowage Plan (SOLAS 1974 regulations VII/4 and VII/7-2 and MARPOL Annex III regulation 5)
45. For oil tankers, the record of oil discharge monitoring and control system for the last ballast voyage (MARPOL Annex I regulation 31.2)
46. Search and rescue cooperation plan for passenger ships trading on fixed routes (SOLAS 1974 regulation V/7.3)
47. For passenger ships, List of operational limitations (SOLAS 1974 regulation V/30.2)
48. Nautical charts and nautical publications (SOLAS 1974 regulations V/19.2.1.4 and V/27)
49. Records of hours of rest and table of shipboard working arrangements (STCW Code section A-VIII/1.5 and 1.7, ILO Convention No.180 Articles 5.7 and 8.1 and MLC 2006 Standards A.2.3.10 and A.2.3.12); and
50. Unattended machinery spaces (UMS) evidence (SOLAS 1974 regulation II-I/46.3).

Part B

List of other certificates and documents which to the extent applicable are required to be on board (as appropriate):

1. Construction drawings (SOLAS 1974 regulation II-1/3-7)
2. Vessel Construction File (SOLAS 1974 regulation II-1/3-10)
3. Manoeuvring booklet and information (SOLAS 1974 regulation II-1/28)
4. Stability information (SOLAS 1974 regulations II-1/5 and II-1/5-1, and LL 1966/LL PROT 1988 regulation 10)
5. Subdivision and stability information (MARPOL Annex I regulation 28)
6. Damage control plans and booklets (SOLAS 1974 regulation II-1/19 and MSC.1/Circ.1245, as amended)
7. Ship Structure Access Manual (SOLAS 1974 regulation II-1/3-6)
8. Enhanced survey report files (in case of bulk carriers or oil tankers) (SOLAS 1974 regulation XI-1/2 and 2011 ESP Code paras 6.2 and 6.3 of annex A, part A and part B, and annex B, part A and part B)

9. Cargo Securing Manual (SOLAS 1974 regulation VI/5.6 and VII/5 and MSC.1/Circ.1353/Rev.1)
10. Bulk carrier booklet (SOLAS 1974 regulations VI/7.2 and XII/8 and BLU Code)
11. Loading/unloading plan for bulk cargoes (SOLAS 1974 regulation VI/7.3)
12. Cargo information (SOLAS 1974 regulations VI/2 and XII/10 and MSC/Circ.663)
13. Fire Control Plan/Booklet (SOLAS 1974 regulations II-2/15.2.4 and II-2/15.3.2)
14. Fire Safety Operational Booklet (SOLAS 1974 regulation II-2/16.2)
15. Fire Safety Training Manual (SOLAS 1974 regulation II-2/15.2.3)
16. Training manual (SOLAS 1974 regulation III/35)
17. Onboard training, drills and maintenance records (SOLAS 1974 regulations II-2/15.2.2.5, III/19.3, III/19.5, III/20.6 and III/20.7)
18. Ship specific plans and procedures for recovery of persons from the water (SOLAS 1974 regulation III/17-1, resolution MSC.346(91) and MSC.1/Circ.1447)
19. Decision support system for masters (passenger ships) (SOLAS 1974 regulation III/29)
20. International Code of Signals and a copy of Volume III of IAMSAR Manual (SOLAS 1974 regulation V/21)
21. Records of navigational activities (SOLAS 1974 regulations V/26 and V/28.1)
22. Ship Security Plan and associated records (SOLAS 1974 regulation XI-2/9 and ISPS Code part A/9 and 10)
23. Engine International Air Pollution Prevention Certificate (NO_x Technical Code 2008 para 2.1.1.1)
24. EEDI Technical File (MARPOL Annex VI regulation 20)
25. Technical Files (NO_x Technical Code 2008 para 2.3.4)
26. Record Book of Engine Parameters (NO_x Technical Code para 2.3.7)
27. Type approval certificate of incinerator (MARPOL Annex VI regulation 16.6)
28. Manufacturer's operating manual for incinerators (MARPOL Annex VI regulation 16.7)
29. Fuel oil changeover procedure (MARPOL Annex VI regulation 14.6)
30. Bunker delivery notes and representative sample (MARPOL Annex VI regulations 18.6 and 18.8.1)
31. Shipboard Oil Pollution Emergency Plan (SOPEP) (MARPOL Annex I regulation 37.1 and resolution MEPC.54(32), as amended by resolution MEPC.86(44))
32. Shipboard Marine Pollution Emergency Plan for Noxious Liquid Substances (MARPOL Annex II regulation 17)
33. Ship Energy Efficiency Management Plan (MARPOL Annex VI regulation 22, MEPC.1/Circ.795)
34. STS operation plan and records of STS operations (MARPOL Annex I regulation 41)

35. Procedures and Arrangements Manual (chemical tankers) (MARPOL Annex II regulation 14.1 resolution MEPC.18(22), as amended by resolution MEPC.62(35))
36. VOC Management Plan (MARPOL Annex VI regulation 15.6)
37. Ballast Water Management Plan (BWM 2004 regulation B-1 and resolution MEPC.127(53), as amended)
38. LRIT conformance test report (SOLAS 1974 regulation V/19-1.6 and MSC.1/Circ.1307)
39. Copy of the certificate of compliance issued by the testing facility, stating the date of compliance and the applicable performance standards of VDR (voyage data recorder) (SOLAS 1974 regulation V/18.8)
40. AIS test report (SOLAS 1974 regulation V/18.9 and MSC.1/Circ.1252)
41. Noise survey report (SOLAS 1974 regulation II-1/3-12)
42. Oil discharge monitoring and control (ODMC) operational manual (MARPOL Annex I regulation 31; resolution A.496(XII); resolution A.586(14), as amended by resolution MEPC.24(22); and resolution MEPC.108(49), as amended by resolution MEPC.240(65))
43. Crude Oil Washing Operation and Equipment Manual (MARPOL Annex I regulation 35 and resolution MEPC.81(43))
44. Material Safety Data Sheets (MSDS) (SOLAS 1974 regulation VI/5-1 and resolution MSC.286(86))
45. Record of AFS (AFS 2001 annex 4 regulation 2)
46. Coating Technical File (SOLAS 1974 regulation II-1/3-2); and
47. Maintenance plans (SOLAS 1974 regulations II-2/14.2.2, II-2/14.3 and II-2/14.4).

For reference:

1. Certificate of Registry or other document of nationality (UNCLOS Article 91)
2. Certificates as to the vessel's hull strength and machinery installations issued by the classification society in question (only to be required if the vessel maintains its class with a classification society)
3. Cargo Gear Record Book (ILO Convention No.32 Article 9.2(4) and ILO Convention No.152 Article 25)
4. Certificates for loading and unloading equipment (ILO Convention No.134 Article 4.3(e) and ILO Convention No.32 Article 9(4))
5. Medical certificates (ILO Convention No.73 or MLC 2006 Standard A1.2)
6. Records of hours of work or rest of seafarers (ILO Convention No.180: part II Article 8.1 or MLC 2006 Standard A.2.3.12)
7. Maritime Labour Certificate (MLC 2006 regulation 5.1.3)

8. Declaration of Maritime Labour Compliance on board (parts I and II) (MLC 2006 regulation 5.1.3)
9. Seafarers' employment agreements (MLC 2006 Standard A 2.1)
10. Certificate of insurance or financial security for repatriation of seafarers (MLC 2006, regulation 2.5); and
11. Certificate of insurance or financial security for shipowners' liability (MLC 2006 regulation 4.2).

The manufacturer's authorised representative in the EU is Springer Nature Customer Service Centre GmbH, Europaplatz 3, 69115 Heidelberg, Germany. If you have any concerns regarding our products, please contact ProductSafety@springernature.com

Printed and bound by CPI Group (UK) Ltd, Croydon, CR0 4YY

26/03/2026

02078916-0012